THE
CASH FLOW
CODE

Six Keys to Unlocking Ultimate Cash Flow

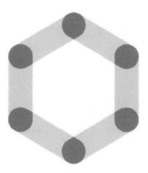

Cliff Spolander

www.businessoptics.co.uk

THE CASH FLOW CODE
Six Keys to Unlocking Ultimate Cash Flow

Copyright ©2020 Cliff Spolander

ISBN: 978-1-9163505-0-2 (paperback)
ISBN: 978-1-9163505-1-9 (ePub)
Also available for Kindle

Layout & pre-press: Lighthouse24

*To my wife, Susie,
and our children, Reuben and Phoebe.*

*I would not have accomplished any of this
were it not for your love and support through
the rollercoaster journey as an entrepreneur.*

This book is for you, with all my love.

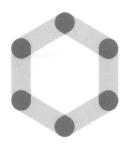

CONTENTS

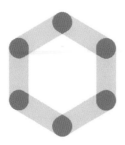

FOREWORD

In my experience the world is divided up between what I call "real-world" people and "non-real-world" people. Cliff is the very essence of a real-world person. He has a wealth of experience across a number of business specialties and is one of that rare breed of person that really understands business and is able to show empathy with business owners. I should know, as I'm a business owner myself.

In 1993, I started the business advisory firm Aspen Waite, aspenwaite.co.uk. Although I had talent and some of the tools I needed to be a success, I was also ill-equipped to face the challenges ahead. How I wish I could have met Cliff and had this book at my disposal at that time...

In the 26 years since starting Aspen Waite, I have developed a degree of wisdom. One thing I am often heard to say is, "When you have money, it's easier to make good decisions, and without money it's much harder." For much of Aspen Waite's life, we struggled with excessive bad debt, and I remember thinking that every year as I grew, all I was doing was creating jobs for others. It's all too easy to get into a wholly reactive culture and convince yourself that if you keep working hard, that's the main thing. But, of course, it isn't.

I think the word "entrepreneur" is bandied about too much, and in reality, most people operate a business devoid of true entrepreneurial spirit. To operate a successful business, you need lots of qualities, but being immersed in your business when you should be working on it is not the answer. Fortunately, for you, the reader, Cliff has expertly laid out in this book how to give yourself the best possible chance to succeed.

Cliff's particular forte lies in cash flow management and optimisation. His knowledge of business is fundamental to this process. In this book, he gets into the heart of cash flow and teaches how to identify costs that can be avoided, minimised, or even increased, with marketing spend being a good example of the latter.

It may be a cliché, but cash really is king. Cash flow is everything. Many profitable businesses have failed because they were not cash generative and/or they didn't implement the right financial model. Please take on the lessons of this book.

If you really want to succeed, you will. You must! I hope you, the reader, appreciate the gift that Cliff is giving you with this book where he lays a clear pathway on how to get the cash flowing in your business, so you reach that success, and peace of mind, you aim for.

Paul Waite
Chief Executive
Aspen Waite Group

OFF THE CASH FLOW ROLLERCOASTER

IF YOU ARE A BUSINESS OWNER, you've likely asked yourself at one time or many times, "Why am I doing this?"

You've likely had the frustrated thought, "It would be easier if I got a job... at least then I'd be guaranteed a consistent income and at the end of the day, I could leave work behind me until the next morning."

Owning a business is, indeed, an emotional and mental roller-coaster. There are the proverbial highs and lows, but at times there seem to be many more lows.

Believe me, as a business owner myself, I've experienced these desperate thoughts and the times of "more lows than highs". Over the past 20 years, I have started, bought, sold, franchised, licensed and systematised several businesses in a variety of sectors, including retail, education, technology, medical, charity and construction.

No matter what business, sector or industry I work in, the two most common areas I find business owners struggle with are cash flow and sustainable business growth. Most people will look outside their business to fix these issues, but as you will discover, my approach is to first look *inside* the business: to look for any cash leaks, tighten up on expenditure and then leverage the current customer base. Once this is done, I look outside the business to grow the customer base and invest in proven marketing strategies to scale the business. Doing this will save both time and money. If you find yourself sceptical about my approach, by the book's end not only will you come to agree with me, but you'll already be starting to enact these systems for increasing the cash flow in your business. That's how potent it is.

Driver or Passenger?

For many of us business owners, a primary reason we started our own business is because we want to be in control of both our own time and income; to have the choice to do the things we want to do and not have to report to anyone. So that's another reason why it's so frustrating when it feels like we're no longer in the driver's seat of our own business, when it feels like our business is running us, rather than us running our business.

For over 20 years, I have found this to be a common occurrence, not only during my own business career but for the business owners with whom I have advised and worked with as well. I experienced this myself in the early years of embarking on my entrepreneurial journey. I was running a successful retail business and, as a very young and naïve 20-year-old, I felt we were doing fairly well.

However, there was a constant struggle to grow or even maintain the cash flow. One day, an invoice would be paid and I would have money in the bank, but the next day, I would pay a supplier and fall into overdraught. As payday drew closer and closer, the more I panicked. I'd be hoping and praying there would be sufficient funds to pay my staff...

Every month was a struggle to keep my head above water. Just as I surfaced to take in air, another wave of outgoings would hit me and I was pulled under, back into overdraught. We were working hard, but every day was a fight. No matter how much effort we put in, the situation didn't change; some months it actually got worse!

Whether they would admit it or not, I'm sure most entrepreneurs have gone through this phase at some point in their journey. Maybe you are there right now?

The fact was, I needed to do something to get my retail business out of this vicious cycle. The management accounts showed that we were a profitable company, but we needed more money. The most logical thing to do was to increase sales. This logic stands to reason: if a business is profitable and needs more money, sales will need to increase.

So we did exactly that. After a mammoth marketing drive for a couple months, sales grew by an average of 20%.

Theoretically, that should have stopped the cash flow rollercoaster we were on. Unfortunately, the increase in sales only made the situation worse! Instead of having more money in the bank account, there was less!

This did not seem logical at all and it left me perplexed, not to mention extremely stressed.

One evening, after the shop closed and everyone left, I was staring at my computer screen, willing the bank balance to go up and wondering what I could do to get out of this mess. After a long while of sheer panic, I had to admit to myself that I did not know how a business truly worked.

There were only two options available to me:

1. To simply quit or keep going until the company died

OR

2. Learn the inner workings of a business and turn my then weakness into a strength.

And so began my journey as an entrepreneur and business owner.

I am pleased to say that we overcame the cash flow problems. It was not easy and many lessons were learnt along the way, the most important of which I share in this book, *The Cash Flow Code*.

Regaining Control with The Cash Flow Code

One of the most common issues I find in working with business owners is the lack of cash flow. In *The Cash Flow Code*, I share the fundamental principles for taking back control of your business and remaining on the front foot, whatever the future brings. I guide you through how to manage your cash and the systems you need to put in place to help you do this.

In this book, we'll delve into the three core financial statements so that you can use them to regain and maintain control of your business and to allow yourself three-way forecasting. These three core statements we'll be working with repeatedly are:

- Balance sheet or statement of financial position

- Profit and loss statement (P&L)

- Cash flow statement

I will also share the seemingly illogical point that, although increasing sales is a key part of the strategy for increasing cash flow, it is the very last key to implement.

As surprising as it might seem, I found from experience that sometimes increasing sales can cause more harm than good. There are five other areas to focus on before any effort is made to increase sales. This may sound counterintuitive, but as you read this book, it will become clear. We explore this surprising strategy through multiple examples because only when you see how the numbers support it, will you become fully convinced and on board.

As you are reading this book, should you have any questions, concerns or you'd like further information and perhaps even assistance in implementing these strategies, please contact me. You can find my contact information and learn more about how I support business owners at my website, www.businessoptics.co.uk.

Your Power Tool

The Cash Flow Simulator is a "power tool" I created for my own businesses and for the companies with whom I consult. It's a tool that allows you to predict what your cash position will be in the next 12 months. This prediction is based firstly upon your company's previous 12 months' performance and secondly, on any changes being implemented in the coming 12 months. In this book, I teach you how to use the Cash Flow Simulator and I provide you with access to it.

With this simulator, my aim is to equip you with the tools and knowledge to constantly monitor, measure and reflect on key areas within your business. Should any one of these areas start to suffer or fail, you will be able to take action quickly to rectify it.

Running a business is like driving a car. As the business owner, you are the driver of the vehicle. As a driver, you have various controls at your disposal: the steering wheel, accelerator, brakes, etc. You also have a dashboard that gives vital information in order to drive the vehicle to your destination safely and on time. It is only from the information outside and on the dashboard that you are able to determine the direction, speed, fuel level, engine temperature and the general health of the vehicle.

Constantly monitoring this information will allow you to make the required adjustments or decide the best course of action to take. Most modern cars not only tell you when you are about to run out of fuel but also if the engine is about to fail, a light is not working or the brake pads are running low. This is vital information to know before it actually breaks down, or worse, fails en route.

The same applies to your business. By constantly monitoring key areas of the business, you can address any problems before they negatively impact your cash flow, profits, customers and team. Within a business, this is a never-ending process. The more you measure, the more adjustments you can make to keep your business running within that ever-moving 'sweet spot'.

The Cash Flow Simulator, along with several other measurements I teach you to use in this book, will allow you to measure and monitor the inner workings of your business. I also show you how to use these tools to identify and adjust potential problem spots. After all, it is better to make dozens of small adjustments than to be forced to make one large, unpredictable correction without knowing exactly what the consequences might be.

Whether you are just embarking on your business journey or you are a long-time entrepreneur, I am convinced that if you put *The*

Cash Flow Code's principles into practice, it will transform how you operate and view your business and even allow you to take back control of it. This book will serve as a guide to help you fulfil your goals and dreams, without making the mistakes that I, and possibly countless others, have made before you.

This all sounds fine in theory, but most important is what it looks like in practice and how it can be applied to your business …

Let's take a look, starting with your business IQ and the "business hexagon"!

BUSINESS IQ

ALTHOUGH PROFIT AND CASH do play a crucial role within a business, we are going to begin our journey into unlocking cash flow by firstly taking a bigger-picture view of the six main aspects at play in a business. We will visit each of these aspects first because getting these areas right will be a strong catalyst to improving both your profit and cash flow.

The Business Hexagon

To illustrate a company, we can use a hexagon. A hexagon is the most efficient, least wasteful shape found in nature—think honeycomb, basalt columns and dragonfly eyes. Within the hexagon, you can find two triangles, which also allows it to be one of the strongest structures in the world.

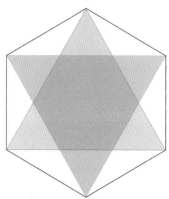

These two triangles represent your business as a whole, recognising the need for firm stability, with the flexibility and adaptability to respond quickly to the ever-changing world in which we live.

The first triangle, standing firmly on its base, represents the core aspects of the company that should not change—culture, people and resources. These are the things on which you can depend whilst everything else around you ebbs and flows.

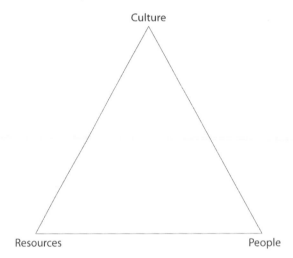

This triangle represents the essence of a company. The culture and environment that staff and customers buy into. It is a place that is stable and dependable, no matter what changes around it.

So how do you create this within your own company?

There are three aspects to this. The first, and most important, is the company's culture, then its people and lastly its resources.

Culture

Many problems within a business can be traced back to its culture.

As a leader and manager of your company, you need to create an environment that fosters mutual respect, encourages forward-thinking and allows everyone the opportunity to express new ideas as well as challenge any old ways of doing things.

I fully appreciate that, when someone criticises something in your business or something you have set up, it can be hard to take. But I urge you to take a step back, remove all emotion and listen to what your people have to say. Weigh it up and, if you feel that the person has a point, test it out… You never know, it could revolutionise your business!

Fostering such an environment encourages people to feel valued and that they have something worth contributing. Allowing them to share and express different ideas and concepts will not only strengthen this core triangle but also feed into the second, more dynamic triangle.

People

Your people are your most valued assets. We will delve deeper into income-generating and cost-saving assets later, but every person you employ must be the right person for the right position at the right time and everyone must work together to pull in the same direction.

This may be a difficult point to address, but it must be done: if anyone in your business is not contributing, they have no place working for you. I know this may sound harsh, but if you do not have everyone aligning to the company's culture and moving in the same direction towards shared goals, it will cause a rift within your team. These rifts are like cancer: they start small, but before you know it, morale has dropped, people are unhappy and ultimately the rate and quality of work will suffer.

Some time ago, I experienced this in one of my companies, a demolition business. I had a young operator who was a good worker and someone I could depend upon. Unfortunately, he had personal problems that started affecting his work. I persevered and worked with him as much as he would allow me. There were times where he did a brilliant job and I felt that there was no way I could let him go. At other times, his attitude and negativity caused other members of staff to leave. In my naiveté, I let this perpetuate for far too long and, by the time I took action, the rot and negativity had affected every team member. I then had to take drastic action to correct it, but unfortunately, my delay in removing him from the team took me over 18 months to rectify.

It is imperative that everyone is aligned to and adopting the culture of the company; individuals who do not want to be part of what the company has to offer must go.

You will find that once the culture is strongly embedded within your company, you will naturally attract people who will align themselves to the values and ethos of the business.

Resources

Resourcing the activities and actions to achieve your goals is vital. There is nothing more demoralizing to people than when they are given a task to do but not the proper resources or tools to help them achieve it. Don't get me wrong, we all need to be resourceful and find solutions to problems and challenges, but there are times that you, as the business owner, cannot expect your team to achieve anything without the proper means.

You can operate an open-door policy, hold regular check-ins with each member of staff, lead from the front or supply the appropriate equipment, etc. I have found that supporting your team in a way that enables them to do the best they can, both professionally and individually, is vital to team morale and overall satisfaction within an organisation.

I was consulting for a charity who were offering specialised services to a very difficult sector of society. Their job could be tough and very emotional. At the time I came on board, each member was expected to use their own personal laptop for work. This was okay for a while, but resentment soon crept in and I found myself caught between unhappy staff and the founders of the charity. With a little persuasion and some energetic fundraising, we got enough money to buy everyone a new laptop. They were by no means the biggest or fastest pieces of kit, but they did the job. The machines were set up and given to each member of staff. This made all the difference: morale increased, as well as work rate and satisfaction.

The same happened in the demolition company I bought a few years ago. When I took over the company, it transpired that the guys had the bare minimum of tools. Not only that, but the equipment was old and unreliable. They were expected to make do and work around any problems they encountered using what they had. Sensing their frustration, I got a range of tools for the various tasks they were carrying out. Admittedly, it did cost a few thousand pounds, but the return on investment was, to a large extent, immeasurable. Team morale increased, work was completed more than 50% faster and customer satisfaction grew.

So the importance of providing, within reason, the correct tools and support will create a solid base from which you can run your business.

Which leads us to the second triangle within our "business hexagon"...

The second triangle is inverted and balanced precariously on its point. This reveals a world that is ever-changing: where technology and the way we work dictate the direction of flow we must embrace.

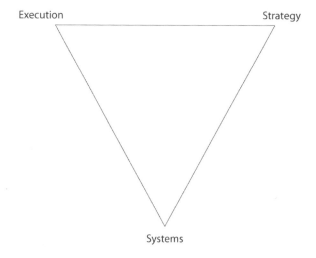

As with everything in life, we must find a balance. You can fool yourself into thinking that nothing changes, but if no effort is made to embrace new methods or technologies, a business will not survive.

An example of this can be seen when Henry Ford invented the motorcar. Those companies making horse-drawn carts or those supplying the companies making horse-drawn carts had to shift and adapt to the new motorcar market. Those that did not simply went out of business.

Even digital marketing has revolutionised how we do business. At the turn of the century, there were only a handful of marketing options open to the average business owner. Nowadays, you can advertise your product or service to anyone in the world for a fraction of what it would have cost a few years back.

In the same way, we cannot go through life thinking everything around us is in constant flux with no fixed reference points. This will cause a lack of focus and security, leading to anxiety and stress. We need to cling to what is firm and unchanging and be open to embrace the things that do change.

As entrepreneurs, we have a responsibility, not only to ourselves but to those with whom we do business—be they employees, customers or clients—to keep firm the core culture of the business but at the same time, to accept that change and innovation, although sometimes a little painful as well as exciting, are a necessary part of business sustainability.

Strategy

This is an area that a lot of businesses struggle with, so I will be covering three specific rules for implementing a strategy.

But firstly, what is strategy?

To answer this I need to ask a further two questions:

1. Who is your client? *Focus on where and how to find them.*

2. How are you going to deliver your product or service? *The key here is to be unique.*

The answers to these two questions will expose your strategy and how you plan to execute your objectives to achieve your goals.

How long will your strategy last? Typically a strategy will be effective for between one to seven years, depending on the sector you are in. Software, for example, is around 18 months.

Another element that should sit behind your strategy to reinforce it is a list of all the things that do NOT align to your strategy. For example: identify the things you are **not** going to do, the clients you are **not** going to engage with, what you are **not** going to create, etc.

The key here is to create a strategy that is emotive and inspires your team.

The 3 Rules for an Effective Strategy

One—be clear on the strategy yourself. If you, as the leader, are unclear about what your company is trying to achieve, then there's no way you can communicate that beyond yourself and no way you can expect your staff to feel secure in your leadership of the organisation. To return to the driver analogy, you need your passengers to trust that you know where you are going!

Two—communicate the strategy in multiple ways. You have got to use every opportunity to communicate the strategy to your staff. Your task here is to align people towards what you want the business to achieve. Create clearly defined roles and goals for each member and formulate a plan of how to achieve what has been set out.

Three—hold people accountable and review the strategy regularly. Be sure to hold people accountable for their role in delivering the company's goals and objectives. Doing this will also allow you to uncover any problems a team member may have, giving you the opportunity to provide support or resources to that individual.

Be proactive in reviewing the overall strategy. The marketplace is an ever-changing environment, so you need to keep your finger on the pulse and ensure that you are ahead of the curve.

Systems

Systems consist of two levels:

1. The Granular Level

2. The Corporate Level

The Granular Level

This is where you focus on systems at the job level. Each and every role within a business needs to be documented and kept in the company's standard operating procedure (SOP) file. The SOP file will be reviewed on a regular basis and kept up to date. The main function of this file is to assist in training new or existing members to take on a particular role within the company. The file also adds value to the business itself, showing potential buyers or investors that the company is robust and not dependent on a particular person and their knowledge in order for it to function.

The Corporate Level

Systemising the business at this level will improve effectiveness and efficiency across the board. Take time to create these systems as they are closely linked with the company's culture.

Examples of Corporate Level Systems

Staff Training	Induction and continuation training
Staff Morale	Team-building days, dynamic meetings, profit or bonus scheme
IT	Software, hardware and online integration and upgrade paths
Financial	Review of regular and detailed financial reports highlighting any potential problems
Plant & Machinery	Regular maintenance and replacement policies
HR & Legal	Outsource externally and have procedures and policies in place

There are many more that could be added to the list, but this gives you some idea of the systems and policies that are required.

Execution

This is where all the working parts of a company start moving and the business becomes a working entity. The working parts are all the elements mentioned in the "business hexagon"—culture, strategy, people, systems and resources.

As a business owner, your job is to constantly monitor the company to see how these parts are performing, making changes where necessary and efficiencies when required.

In order to do this, we must **T-E-S-T**:

Test	Test and measure using key performance indicators (KPIs). Test all systems and processes within the business to see how they are performing.
Efficiencies	Examine and analyse both the internal and external factors that influence your industry and make efficiencies where required.
Surround	Create a team within your business to drive the company forward. Also create a team of specialists outside of your business that you can call upon when required.
Time Out	Take time to reward your team and to celebrate wins that are achieved over a period of three to six months.

I hope this chapter has shown that a business is more than simply about making money. It demonstrates what an amazing responsibility we have as business owners to serve the people working for us and to serve the wider community. By doing so, we enrich not only ourselves but the people around us, which is precisely what we are called to be and do.

Now that we have covered the basic fundamentals underpinning a business—culture, people, resources, strategy, systems and execution—next we will focus on your financial IQ: the three core financial statements to better understand three-way forecasting and to get a handle on how a business functions financially.

Quick-Fire Action Points

- How strong are your two triangles?

- What culture have you created, or are you creating, within your business?

- What type of person is your business attracting?

- Are you providing sufficient resources to your team?

- Have you clearly defined and communicated your strategy?

- Are the systems within your business sufficient, or do they need some work?

- How well are all the moving parts working? Do you need to do some tinkering?

3 FINANCIAL IQ

THERE ARE THREE KEY BENEFITS of increasing your financial intelligence. By developing a deeper understanding of your company's financials, you will also be able to:

1. Critically assess your company.

As a business owner it is vital to be able to answer questions like:
- Do I have enough cash to make payroll?
- Do I know how profitable my products or services are?

2. Read between the numbers.

Management accounts are not always what they seem. Having the ability, knowledge and confidence to interpret and question the data will enable you to take the most effective action.

3. Make informed decisions.

To lead your company in the correct direction, answers to the return on investment (ROI) of a project, as well as when, why and how to spend money, must be answered.

The Three Core Statements

Every business owner should be operating with these three core financial statements to enable three-way forecasting:
1. Balance sheet or statement of financial position
2. Profit and loss statement (P&L)
3. Cash flow statement

You may be feeling a little daunted by financial statements. Don't worry; I did too at the start. When I started out in business, knowing how to read financial statements was challenging, not to mention trying to work out what they were telling me or how they all fitted and worked together to create meaningful and useable information with which to grow my business.

I had questions like:

- What part of the balance sheet do I need to look at?

- Which numbers are important?

- How do these numbers reveal the health of my business?

It took me a long time to work this out and even then, as my financial IQ increased, my available time decreased. I spent more of my time running the operational end of my business, which didn't allow me time to study these documents in order to gain a proper understanding of what the numbers were telling me about the financial health of my business.

As time went on, all I wanted was to see, in a matter of seconds, was a single document that immediately told me which areas of my business were on track and which areas needed attention. I didn't have time to make sense and interpret all the numbers every time I checked my finances. And so began my quest to find the key parts of the balance sheet, profit and loss (P&L) statement and cash flow statement that I could take to create a dashboard for my businesses.

Over the course of this book, I will reveal which numbers are important. By the book's end I will share how to turn these numbers into meaningful information that will allow you to start creating your own cash flow forecast, with the formulas needed to build a successful business. Knowing this information will help you to keep control over your cash flow, understand how to fix problems when they arise and be able to make informed decisions. This will ultimately enable you to drive your business forward and ensure it is operating at optimum efficiency.

As a business owner, it is your responsibility to develop your understanding of these key number in order to analyse how they relate to the activities within your business.

Most business owners receive their set of management accounts once a year. They take a quick glance to check whether they made a profit or a loss. Then they carry on going about their business for another year. I know, because I did that myself. With the change in online accounting software, accessing your company's management accounts could not be easier. You should ideally be looking at your management accounts every month or at least every quarter. By constantly checking the key figures, you will begin to see trends, allowing you to take corrective action should those trends start to deviate negatively. This all contributes to increasing your financial IQ.

Time

There is another key fundamental here that is not immediately obvious when looking at management accounts. This key is what we use to benchmark how well your business is doing and it allows us to create trends and meaning between numbers. This key fundamental is—time.

Using time, we can create trends and measure the connection between the numbers for a set time period. It is only by studying trends and comparing financial reports over time that we find the information needed to fix any problems that may be lurking under the bonnet.

But let's not run away with ourselves! Firstly, it is vital that we gain an understanding of what financial statements are. Otherwise, your success will only be half-baked. In the rest of this chapter, I'll help you gain a good understanding of these three core financial statements.

Balance Sheet/Statement of Financial Position

What is a balance sheet and how can I interpret one?

BALANCE SHEET

ASSETS	LIABILITIES
THINGS YOU OWN	THINGS YOU OWE
	EQUITY
	BALANCE

In short, a balance sheet is simply a list of things you *own* against a list of things you *owe*.

As a business owner, you will have assets and liabilities in various forms. It's the balance sheet that summarises your company's assets, liabilities and shareholders' equity at a particular point in time. The left-hand column, the assets (things you own), must equal the sum of the right-hand column, the liabilities (things you owe) and the equity (balance).

For example, if a business owner has borrowed £10K from the bank (a liability) and has had £10K invested by its shareholders (shareholder equity), then the business has £20K of cash at its disposal (an asset).

Assets

What is classed as an asset?

From an accountancy point of view, there are many things that would be classed as assets. A common way of categorising them is to split them between current assets (assets that can be turned into cash quickly) and fixed or non-current assets (assets that would take some time to turn into cash).

The accountancy definition of an asset is a resource that is controlled by a business as a result of a past event that will bring economic benefits to the business.

In chapter 4, we will be looking at the entrepreneur's definition of an asset.

Current assets can include:
- Cash and other things that are similar to cash, such as certificates of deposits (CDs) or treasury shares
- Accounts receivables, or money owed to you which you can chase to get paid
- Inventory, which is stock that you can sell

Non-current assets can include:
- Land, buildings, equipment, machinery and other big capital expenditure items
- Intangible things, like intellectual property
- Investments that have a time limit/restriction on when they can be cashed in

Liabilities

What is a liability?

Liabilities are things that the business owes and, like assets, they can be classified as either current liabilities or non-current liabilities. The definition of a liability is a present obligation arising from past events, which is expected to result in an outflow of economic resources from the business.

Current liabilities can include:
- Bank overdrafts
- Interest payable
- Operational costs like rent or utilities
- Tax
- Salaries for your staff
- Dividends

Non-current liabilities can include:
- Pension fund contributions
- Deferred tax
- Debts due in more than one year's time

Equity

What is shareholder equity?

Shareholder equity is made up of:
- Investments by shareholders (equity)
- Retained earnings—this is generally not cash that is available; this is simply the cumulative profits made by the business over its lifetime
- Current earnings—the current profit/loss of the business (explained in the P&L statement)

What Does It All Mean?

A balance sheet is a snapshot in time of what a business looks like. This is because the numbers that form part of a balance sheet are constantly changing.

Because of this snapshot, it's important to compare balance sheets over time. In terms of reading the balance sheet, there are a number of ratios that can be used to give business owners greater insight. Let's look at two of those ratios: debt-to-equity ratio and current ratio.

Debt-to-Equity Ratio — total liabilities divided by total equity

A business that has a high debt-to-equity ratio is described as "highly geared" or "highly leveraged", which makes it less attractive to lenders.

The ratio can never be perfect as it can depend on industry-wide factors. If you are running a comparison, then do so against comparable businesses in the same industry. The kind of questions owners should ask are:

- Are the business's sales predictable and generating cash?

- Are the debts likely to be repaid quickly?

- Is the business vulnerable to economy factors?

BALANCE SHEET

Current Assets	**CURRENT RATIO:**	**Current Liabilities**
Cash in Bank		Accounts Payable
Short-Term Investments		Unpaid Dividends
Accounts Receivable		Loans/Interest
Tax Refunds	*Current Assets*	Money Due
Interest Receiveable	*alway want*	Wages/Commissions
Pre-Paid Expenses	*to be greater than*	
Stock/Inventory	*Current Liabilities*	

Non-Current Assets
Equipment
(*less depreciation*)
Buildings/Land
(*less depreciation*)

Intangible Assets
Copyright
Goodwill
Trademarks
Patent Rights

Other Assets
Money Owed to
the Company

Investments
Bonds
Insurances
Land
Stocks

Non-Current Liabilities
Bonds/Mortgages
Loans Payable

Other Liabilities
Pension Obligations
Deferered Income
Loans > 3 years

TOTAL LIABILITIES

DEBT TO EQUITY RATIO:

Total Liabilities /
Total Equity

This needs to be as small as possible

Equity
Capital Stock
Retained /
Current Earnings
Treasury Stocks
Net Income

TOTAL EQUITY

TOTAL ASSETS

=

TOTAL LIABILITIES + EQUITY

Current Ratio — current assets divided by current liabilities

This is a relatively quick and easy approach to calculating whether a business is likely to be able to meet its short-term requirements and pay its bills.

A ratio of more than one would indicate that if a firm's total obligations became due immediately, the business could pay them with funds they had available. The business would not need to raise alternative funds, such as a loan or share issue.

The Profit and Loss (P&L) Statement

The profit and loss (P&L) statement for a business contains information about how well it's doing.

In its most simple form, the P&L tells you how much you have sold, how much you have bought and how much profit (or loss) you have made during a specific period of time.

The P&L is a relatively easy document to interpret, which is why it tends to be the first one that many people look at when assessing the health of a business.

But it is important to understand its limitations. The P&L will not tell you about the underlying health of the business, such as how much money it owes or is owed and what the value of its assets are.

The P&L will show you whether a business is making a profit but not whether it is generating cash.

NOTE: please remember profit and cash are not the same thing. A business can be highly profitable, but if it fails to convert those profits into cash, the whole enterprise is worthless.

This difference between profit and cash flow will be discussed in more detail in chapter 6: Understanding Cash Flow.

Each P&L is time-specific. It shows the performance of a business for a set period of time, which could be a week, a month or a year.

The Five Main Sections of a P&L

Most P&L statements are put together in a similar way, although the detail of what is included in each section may vary from one business to another.

1. Turnover

Turnover, revenue or sales is the total value of what the business has sold during the period covered by the P&L statement, net of VAT if applicable. It might be broken down into different types of products, helping you to see which items sell better than others.

Other income received by the business, such as bank interest or money received from the sale of assets, is not included in turnover because it does not represent income from your main trading activity.

2. Cost of Sales

These are the costs that are directly related to the sales you have made. It includes raw materials or stock purchased to resell. It may also include the cost of creating the items that you sold, including the cost of wages if you are selling services.

3. Gross Profit

Gross profit is the sum of turnover minus cost of sales. It tells you how much profit you are making directly from your sales.

4. Expenses or Operating Costs

These are all the other costs associated with running a business, such as the rent and rates on your premises, staff costs, accountancy, legal fees, depreciation, etc. These costs cannot be directly linked to your sales and may not change much, even if your sales figures were to change significantly.

5. Net Profit

Net profit is the gross profit minus the operating costs. You could think of it as the true profit of your business because it comprises all the income and all the costs associated with running the business. This isn't the profit that you will pay tax on because taxable profit is calculated slightly differently, but it's probably not far off that figure.

Cash Flow Statement

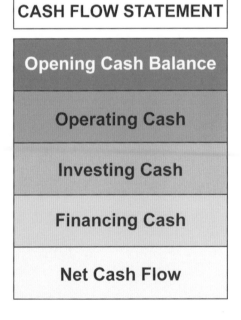

A cash flow statement describes how the cash flows in and out of the business.

The cash flow statement is often considered less important than the balance sheet and P&L. However, it is this statement that shows trends in business performance that cannot be seen by reading the other two financial statements.

As profit and cash are not the same beast, there can be significant differences between the results shown in the P&L and the cash flow statement.

Not all cash is the same. Within the cash flow statement, you have three sources of cash:

Operating Cash—broadly speaking, operating cash refers to the sales generated from business activities to pay for expenses and business overheads.

Investing Cash—this entails payments made to purchase and sell certain assets, such as plant, machinery, or vehicles.

Financing Cash—this is cash generated from borrowing from a bank or by selling company shares. It can be used as a payment of dividends to shareholders or to repay money to a bank.

There can be significant differences between the results shown in the P&L statement and the cash flow statement. The main reason (but certainly not the only reason) is due to time. This will be explained later in the chapter when we look at cash accounting vs. accrual accounting.

As an investor, and certainly when I am looking to purchase a company, the cash flow statement is the main document I inspect because it is the most transparent of all the financial statements. It shows the true performance of the business and highlights any potential cash flow problems during the business's financial cycle. It is also the least likely of the statements to be misleading as it is simply a reflection of the company's bank account.

How It All Fits Together

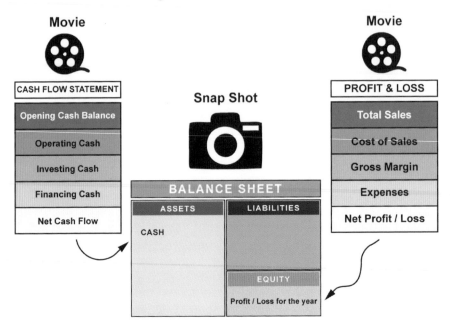

The cash flow statement is a dynamic document, like a movie, playing out for certain time periods—be it monthly, quarterly or yearly. It tells you what happened to the *cash in the business* during that period of time. This figure is then the number reported in the balance sheet as *cash* under the *assets* column.

The P&L statement is similar to the cash flow statement in that it is also dynamic, a movie. It tells the story of the *total sales and expenses* during that period of time. This figure is then the number reported in the balance sheet as *profit* for the year under the *equity* column.

The balance sheet is static, a photograph if you will, of the business at a particular point in time. A balance sheet is, therefore, a snapshot of what the company looks like at the start of the financial year. The cash flow and P&L movie starts to play for the 12-month period and at the end of the financial year, another balance sheet is produced, giving another picture of what the business looks like 12 months down the line.

Power comes when a business owner understands and compares all these statements to get a clear and true picture of their business's health.

Another way of looking at this is as follows:

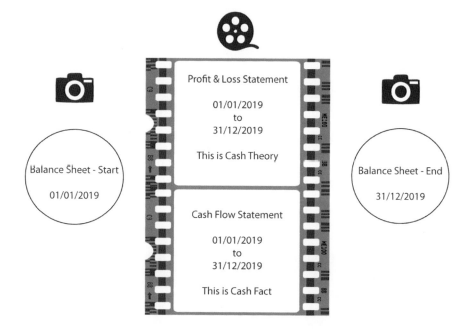

The three financial statements are there to show us the key pieces of information we need to keep our business on track:

Balance Sheet—this tells you about the assets (*things you own*), the liabilities (*things you owe*) and the equity (*balance*) at a certain point in time.

Profit & Loss Statement—this tells you whether or not your sales are greater than your expenses, irrespective of when cash was exchanged.

Cash Flow Statement—this is not accounting theory but real events. It keeps track of the flow of money in your account, highlighting any potential risks throughout the company's financial cycle.

This will be discussed further in chapter 5, where I show you the trends and ratios needed to keep track of your business's health. These trends and ratios are taken from the balance sheet, P&L statement and cash flow statement so that you can calculate how your business is performing. The figures can then be used to compare how your business has performed in the past, as well as to check how it is doing in comparison to the industry averages.

Cash vs. Accrual Accounting

To keep track of a business's activities, there are really only two viable options available—cash accounting or accrual accounting.

The difference between cash accounting and accrual accounting comes down to one thing: timing.

When do you record revenue or expenses?

If it is recorded when you pay or receive money, this is cash accounting. If you record it when you get a bill or raise an invoice, it is accrual accounting.

If the purpose of accounting is to keep track of the company's activities and to create an accurate picture, the only option is accrual accounting.

Let's explore this a little further...

Cash Accounting

Cash accounting only records activities within the business when, and only when, there is a cash transaction, i.e., when cash enters or leaves the bank account.

Advantages: it is simple and shows how much money you have on hand. It is an easier option for calculating tax, though not all businesses are allowed to use it. Check out the HMRC website for specifics.

Since each financial transaction is supported by the exchange of cash, the accounts require less analysis. Activities do not appear in the financial records unless the company receives or makes a payment.

Disadvantages: due to the way that cash accounting works, the business owner needs to invest a lot of time to working out which activities occurred during which month. It is misleading because this method could, at a certain time, show the business as profitable, but this may be just because the purchase invoices and bills have not yet all been paid.

Accrual Accounting

This method records the sales and expenditure relating to that month or period of time, regardless of whether cash exchanges hands.

Accrual accounting records the activities the business undertook for that period. In other words, it only records the transactions—sales and expenses—for that period and does not take into account what is happening in the bank account.

For example, if the company earned revenue during the current month, this revenue appears on the P&L statement. The company may not receive payment until the following month, but it has recorded that the company engaged in income-producing activities during the current month.

To explain this another way, let's visit an example.

Scenario

ABC Ltd purchased £3,000.00 worth of stock in January. It raised two sales invoices, £3,000.00 and £2,000.00. The monthly overhead in January, including wages, came to £750.00.

The £3,000.00 worth of stock must be paid within 30 days. The sales invoice of £3,000.00 was paid in February, but the other invoice of £2,000.00 had to be chased and was only paid in March. If we assume, for simplicity's sake, that there were no further sales and expenses/overheads after January, the following would be recorded:

Cash Accounting

	January	February	March
Sales	£0.00	£3,000.00	£2,000.00
Cost of Sales	£3,000.00	£0.00	£0.00
Expenses	£750.00	£0.00	£0.00

Therefore, according to cash accounting, in January there would be a £3,750.00 loss, in February a £3,000.00 profit and in March a £2,000.00 profit.

Accrual Accounting

	January	February	March
Sales	£5,000.00	£0.00	£0.00
Cost of Sales	£3,000.00	£0.00	£0.00
Expenses	£750.00	£0.00	£0.00

Accrual accounting will show a profit of £1,250.00 for January: a more accurate version of events.

Using this method allows you to generate accurate business optics. Having accurate optics means you can see what is truly happening in your business, on a month-by-month basis, giving you exact trends and cycles within the business and allowing you to strategically plan ahead based upon precise information.

Accrual accounting also allows you to take a lump sum payment, such as business insurance, and record this expense over the 12 months of trading, thus giving a more accurate and realistic view of what is actually happening in the business. However, from a cash perspective, the full 12 months' worth of insurance costs would be leaving the bank account in one payment.

In short, accrual accounting is more accurate but requires careful cash flow management. Cash accounting is an easier way of recording the activities of a business but does not reflect the reality of how a business is performing, which if relied upon could skew the information and thus lead to poor decision-making.

In this chapter, we have covered the three core financial statements and how they work together. However, it is only by comparing these financial statements over time that we can then start to see trends and gather useful information. We have also explored the differences between cash and accrual accounting, considering the advantages and disadvantages of each. Now that we have a good financial overview, it is time to delve deeper and take a look at assets and expenses to see how they affect your performance, profitability and cash flow.

Quick-Fire Action Points

- How often do you look at your management accounts?

- Do you know the cash position of your business at the moment?

- Is your business operating cash accounting or accrual accounting?

- What could you do over the next three months to improve your financial IQ?

4   ASSETS AND EXPENSES

IN THIS CHAPTER, we will discover what an entrepreneur defines as an asset and how quickly expenses can impact, not only profits, but also how quickly it will affect cash flow. I will give you a few examples of assets and expenses as well as four rules you can use to get expenses back under control. Getting a handle on this area of your business will enable you to maximise profits and, at the same time, improve cash flow.

What Is an Asset?

Asset – "an item of property owned by a person or company, regarded as having value and available to meet debts, commitments, or legacies" (from *Oxford Dictionaries*).

Or in other words: an asset is a resource that is controlled by a business as a result of a past event that will bring economic benefits to the business.

Examples of assets: cash, investments, accounts receivable, inventory, supplies, land, buildings, equipment and vehicles.

According to American businessman and writer Robert Kiyosaki, an asset is "anything that puts money in your pocket".

Our success as entrepreneurs is in our ability to find and invest in assets that generate an income: "things that put money in our pockets".

Entrepreneur's Definition of an Asset

I would like to take Robert Kiyosaki's definition one step further because, during my time as a business owner and consultant, I have found the definition of an asset to be anything that puts money into my pocket, as well as anything that *stops money from leaving my pocket*. We also need to ensure and monitor what sort of return on profits and operating cash flow these assets are producing.

For these reasons, I have come to the conclusion that assets can be classed as either *income-generating assets* or *cost-saving assets*.

Income-generating assets are the things that put money in your pocket (Robert Kiyosaki's interpretation). Income-generating assets can be employees, machinery, products you sell, anything that generates a net profit for you.

Think of your business assets as little money-generators that produce income for you. As a business owner, you need to be constantly watching these engines and fine-tuning them so that they produce the best possible margins for you.

For every £, $ or € you invest, there must be a return greater than that which you spent. Therefore, you need to measure how much each asset costs against the income it generates.

Cost-saving assets are things that reduce expenses, time or overheads that support income-generating assets, which, in turn, will reduce the amount of money leaving your pocket.

Cost-saving assets may be as simple as buying a guillotine rather than a small pair of scissors if your business involves cutting paper. Or it may be a more reliable laptop that does not crash four times a day, requiring painstaking re-starting and recovery of work. Anything that will reduce time and optimise your business's efficiency at making profit can be classed as a cost-saving asset.

These two types of assets work hand-in-hand. As business owners, we must always look for assets that produce an income but, at the same time, we must constantly look for ways to reduce the drag that overheads and expenses have on our profit margins.

How do we do this?

1. Place an income value against every income asset.
2. Put an expense reduction value against every cost-saving asset.
3. Remove or improve underperforming assets.
4. Find technology or people to reduce expenses and overheads.

Let us use these four points in a practical example, using the demolition business that I used to own.

1—Place an income value against every income-generating asset.

I created a spreadsheet for every project my team undertook. In this spreadsheet, I would record the following:

- Number of days worked

- Number of man-days worked

- Number of man-hours worked

- Labour Costs

- Other Costs:
  - Skips
  - Hire Equipment
  - Equipment Bought
  - Stay & Travel
  - Fuel
  - Bonuses
  - Agency Labour Costs

The spreadsheet looked something like the next page:

Order Value	£	7,380.77	28.65%
Labour Cost	£	2,114.40	20.56%
Other Cost	£	1,517.61	
Gross Profit	£	3,748.76	
Gross Margin		50.79%	

ROI	£	2.03

Client	Client ABC Ltd
Project	Project 1
Start Date	14/01/2019
End Date	18/01/2019
Number of Phases	1

		T/O per day		GP per day		
Number of Calendar Days	5	£ 1,476.15	£	749.75	per man day
Number of Man Days	24	£ 307.53	£	156.20	per man day
Number of Man Hours	192	£ 38.44	£	19.52	per man hour

Week 1

	Monday 14-Jan	Tuesday 15-Jan	Wednesday 16-Jan	Thursday 17-Jan	Friday 18-Jan	Hours	Hourly cost		Cost for week	
Foreman	8	8	8	8	8	40	£	15.66	£	626.40
Labourers (1)	8		8	8	8	32	£	11.50	£	368.00
Labourers (2)	8	8	8	8	8	40	£	9.50	£	380.00
Labourers (3)	8	8	8	8	8	40	£	9.00	£	360.00
Labourers (4)	8	8	8	8	8	40	£	9.50	£	380.00
Labourers ()						0	£		£	-
Labourers ()						0	£		£	-
Labourers ()						0	£		£	-
								TOTAL	£	2,114.40	£11.01 ph

	Skips		Hire		Equipment		Hotel		Labour	
	£	372.80	£	84.00						
	£	664.88	£	168.00						
	£	138.24								
	£	1,175.92	£	252.00	£	-	£	-	£	-

Other Costs

Fuel	£	89.69
Skips	£	1,175.92
Hire	£	252.00
Equipment	£	-
Hotel	£	-
Labour	£	-
Bonus		
TOTAL	£	1,517.61
	£	7.90

From the spreadsheet, it is easy to see the following information at a glance:

- The average hourly rate I paid my operatives equalled £11.01 per hour.
- The hourly burn rate of all the other costs—skips, hire equipment, etc.—came in at £7.90/man-hour.
- The turnover generated was £38.44/man-hour.
- The gross profit rate was at £19.52/man-hour.
- The total turnover, expenses and gross profit equated to £7,380.77, £3,632.01 and £3,748.76 respectfully.
- The return on investment (ROI)—for every £1 I spent, I received £2.03.

As you can see, every person on my team is measured in terms of what I pay (wages) against what income they generate (sales). In this example, the average hourly cost to me is £11.01 per hour and my return in sales is £38.44 per hour.

I can immediately see that for every £1.00 I spent on this project, I produced £2.03 in return. Therefore, my investment of £3,632.01 for the whole project produced a return of £7,380.77 in five days or £3,748.76 in gross profit.

Recording this information enables me to ensure my wages and expenses do not spiral out of control on a project. Over time, I have built up very good averages, so I can now predict, to a high degree of accuracy, how long a project should take and what my other costs are likely to be. By taking the time to understand these numbers and record them, I've empowered myself to better control my projects rather than be at their mercy. By following this practice, you too can achieve the same in your business.

2—Put an expense reduction value against every cost-saving asset.

This is less easy to record. It will depend largely on the type of business you run and will rely on some common sense and financial IQ.

Let us take another easy but real-life example. I had a project that required a large amount of block walls to be taken down. There were two options available to me:

1. Use all four operatives for a six-day period and have them take the walls down by hand. This would equate to an average of £11 per hour wages x 8 hours per day x 4 operatives x 6 days, which worked out to £2,112.00 in labour costs for the project.

OR

2. I could use three operatives for only three days but hire a digger to take the walls down. This would equate to an average of £11 per hour wages x 8 hours per day x 3 operatives x 3 days, plus the hire of the digger at £495.00. This worked out to £1,287.00 for the project.

Therefore, option 2 was the more profitable option. In this situation, the digger was a cost-saving asset because, although it cost me £495.00 to hire it, I made a savings of £825.00 and was also able to better-utilise my remaining operatives on another project.

The same could be said for a salesperson with an old laptop that is slow and keeps crashing. If you were paying them £25 per hour and, due to the crashes and having to wait for the laptop to reboot, they were wasting an average of two hours per day, you would effectively be wasting £50 per day. It would make good financial sense to replace the laptop, which may cost around £800.00–£1000.00, but would be recouped within the first month of increased productivity, not to mention the extra sales they will make, combined with a happier, less frustrated employee.

Putting an expense reduction value against every cost-saving asset will highlight areas that could be improved, for example:

- Is it worth keeping an old company vehicle that keeps breaking down or is it better to replace it with a more reliable and efficient vehicle?

- Could the building you are currently using be better configured to improve productivity or, even better still, be sub-let to provide an income?

- Do you have a process within the business that could be automated using software or contracted out?

Addressing these areas within your business will have a direct impact on profits and create a more efficient company.

3—Remove or improve underperforming assets.

As in the example above, replacing the laptop improved the under-performing "cost-saving" asset, thus making the salesperson more productive.

The same can be said for staff: if team members are underperforming, they either need further training and support to help them progress to where they need to be or a discussion would need to take place in order to ascertain if this is the right position for them or whether they may need to consider moving on.

Stock is also considered an asset as it is something you have bought and will be selling, hopefully, for more than its cost price. However, the longer it sits on the shelf, the more it is soaking up cash that could be invested elsewhere. In this instance, it would be better to sell the old stock at cost price in order to recoup the money so that it can be invested in stock that moves quickly, allowing your money to work and grow. In turn, your stress and worry decrease as your sense of control increases.

4—Find technology or people to reduce expenses and overheads.

Nowadays, with the internet and technology moving at such a fast pace, there is bound to be something or someone to whom you could subcontract a task.

- Cloud-based computing has done away with having an onsite server and a dedicated IT person or company looking after it all for you.
- Virtual PAs and office hire reduces the need to take on a

permanent member of staff or building lease. You only pay for what you use or need with a pay-as-you-go service.

- As the sales and marketing process is evolving all the time and getting increasingly more complex, it may pay to contract this out to a specialist third party who, in this competitive market, will need to guarantee results in order to retain you as their customer.

There are so many options out there. It is worth taking some time out of your business to really assess which areas in your company can be streamlined, which assets need some tweaking and how can you reduce expenditure. When you make time to reflect, evaluate and plan, you put yourself firmly in the driver's seat of your business, resulting in an increased sense of control that all business owners need.

If you would like help and support to work through this process, I would be pleased to work alongside you. Please feel free to email me at hello@businessoptics.co.uk and I will be happy to arrange a phone call with you.

Hidden Dangers of Expenses

Expenses and overspending are often the demise of a business. Having mastery over your spending habits will result in more profits and better cash flow.

We will look at the impact expenses have on a company's profit in chapter 6. For now, here are four rules I use in my own businesses to help me to stay focused and to keep my cash flow in check, which then helps me feel in control of my business and not at its mercy.

Rule #1 Remove Emotion

At one time or another, we all get seduced by the option to supersize or upgrade from what we originally intended to buy. Take a vehicle or computer, for example. There is always a temptation to add an extra package here, a bigger hard drive there, etc. After all, you work hard and deserve a little luxury now and again, right? WRONG!

There is a lot of power behind delayed gratification.

At the early stages of wealth creation, you cannot afford to make this mistake. You must have a laser-like focus and spend your time and energy investing all you can into creating the lifestyle you want in the future. Only once you achieve your goals, can you pat yourself on the back and have that little luxury you always wanted.

Expense rule #3 (below) will show you how to work out the true cost of items you buy. Using this formula before making any purchase will open your eyes to how a little extra spending here and there causes catastrophic problems for profits and cash flow.

Rule #2 SOS—Stop Over-Spending

Once you have rule #1 in check, you can begin to control your spending. The number one question to always ask yourself is, "Will this money I am about to spend give me a return?"

Will a computer with some extra RAM and a bigger screen make you more money than a slightly smaller model? If the answer is no, then you don't need it. Will a good quality office chair and desk from a charity shop make you less money than a brand-new one costing four times as much? Probably not.

The temptation to go for something slightly bigger, better, newer is always out there... BUT if that something does not make a positive difference to your bottom line and cash flow, then leave it alone. You simply do not need it! (See rule #1!)

Before buying anything, ask yourself the questions in expense rule #4.

Rule #3 Work Out the True Cost

People have labelled compound interest the 8th Wonder of the World. I like to think that calculating the true cost of a business expense is the 9th Wonder!

The price at which you see the product advertised is rarely, if ever, the price you really pay.

Let's consider a real-life example:

> You need a new printer and there is one you like on sale for only £299.99 excluding VAT. You whip out the bank card and, a few clicks later, the printer is ordered and delivered the next day.
>
> Now to work out the true cost of this printer: let us assume your net profit is 10%, meaning that, for every £100.00 of sales made, you generate £10.00 in net profit.
>
> The printer costs £299.99; therefore, in order for the business to pay for the printer, it must produce £299.99 worth of profit.
>
> If the net profit is 10%, the business must make sales of £2,999.90 to pay for the printer. Therefore, the true cost of the printer is not £299.99 but £2,999.90!

I first discovered this during my early years in business. Cash flow was always a problem and, even though I knew we were spending a little here and there, it was never large amounts. It wasn't until I looked at the relationship between percentage of net profit and sales, that it dawned on me that with only 8% net profit, everything we spent was in reality over 12.5 times more than the price it was actually bought for. Only then did I realise that every £, $ or € I spent must either bring me a return or help reduce my outgoings.

Rule #4 Ask the 7 Emotion-Expulsion Questions

To help remove all emotion from spending, ask yourself these seven emotion-expulsion questions:

1. Have I used the TRUE COST formula?

2. Will this make me money?

3. Will this purchase create wealth?

4. Will it reduce my costs and drive profits?

5. Do I really need the top-of-the-range or will the standard version be okay?

6. Can I delay purchasing this for 24 hours?

7. Can I delay the purchase for another week? (If you can, you probably don't need it!)

Now that you know what an entrepreneur's definition of an asset is, you can start to discover what assets are in your business. By constantly monitoring both types of assets, you can keep your business running as efficiently as possible. We have also explored the four rules of expenses. Being able to control your business's expenses will have a big impact on both profits and cash flow.

In the next chapter, we discover which numbers in your three financial statements are most important and how they fit together to create meaningful information over time. By following these numbers, you best position yourself to know when your business is doing well and when something is going in the wrong direction, knowledge that allows you to make the best decisions for your business.

Quick-Fire Action Points

- Assess all income-generating assets.

- Assess all cost-saving assets.

- Track the performance of each service or product.

- Look to reduce expenses as much as possible.

- Calculate the true cost of purchases for your business.

5

RATIOS AND TRENDS

In this chapter, we will look at which ratios and trends you will need to measure so that you can see if something in your business is starting to suffer. These ratios include your return on sales (ROS), asset turnover, return on assets (ROA), profit control and cash control. Regularly determining these ratios supplies you with critical information, information that will act like an early warning system, alerting you to potential problems—the same way your car warns you when the fuel is running low.

By calculating these ratios over time and comparing the results to your past performance and that of your industry, you will be able to create this early warning system bespoke to your own business.

Before going into the calculations, it is important to point out that we need to compare like for like. The only way we can do this is to use percentages. This is known as common sizing.

Return on Sales (ROS) or Profit Margin

Return on sales (ROS), also referred to as the operating profit margin, is a ratio used to evaluate a company's operational efficiency in generating profits from its sales. In other words, it measures a company's performance by analysing what percentage of total sales are converted into profits.

For your ROS to carry meaning for you, it needs to be compared to both the industry you are in and how you have performed in the past.

Here is the formula for determining your ROS:

$$ROS = \frac{Net\ Profit}{Sales}$$

What happens if the trend of your ROS is below market average or going in the wrong direction? There are two potential problems you may have:

1. *Sales Problem:* are your sales increasing faster than inflation? If not, this could be the reason.

2. *Profit Problem:* if your sales are growing, it may be that your gross margin is decreasing or expenses are increasing quicker than your sales.

Asset Turnover

$$Asset\ turnover = \frac{Sales}{Assets}$$

Asset turnover is a measure of how your assets are performing in terms of sales. You can increase asset turnover by either increasing sales while keeping assets steady or by decreasing assets while keeping sales steady.

A high asset turnover translates into a higher return on assets (ROA) and is an indication of how efficiently a company is at using its assets. A lower asset turnover indicates inefficiency and potential internal problems within the company. So whether your asset turnover is high or low, it provides you valuable feedback.

Return on Assets (ROA)

For the return on assets (ROA), first I'll explain how to calculate it and then how to use this calculation to determine if there are problems in your business. The way to calculate the ROA is as follows: take the assets found on the balance sheets from the beginning and end of the period and divide by two. This gives you the average asset value.

$$\text{Average Assets} = \frac{(bA + eA)}{2}$$

(bA = beginning assets)
(eA = ending assets)

Then take the net profit and divide it by the average asset value.

$$\text{ROA} = \frac{\text{Net Profit}}{\text{Average Assets}}$$

Return on assets shows how the assets in your business are performing. If the return on assets are not at least the same as the industry standard or have been declining over time, you may have a return on asset problem.

If your numbers indicate a problem, in order to fix it, you will need to look in the following places:

- In the accounts **receivable, payable** and **inventory,** check the trends over time in terms of days—both debtor days and creditor days. If the average debtor days begin increasing, this will indicate that you are not getting paid on time or stock levels are increasing. If creditor days are decreasing, it will indicate that you are paying suppliers too quickly.

- If these ratios and trends are ideal, look at the **cash balance.** It could indicate that there is too much money in the bank account and not enough is being invested in growing the business. Investments you could make to grow the business might include the acquisition of other income-generating or cost-saving assets, or even the acquisition of another business.

- If that is not the problem, then we need to look at the **fixed assets** within the business.

Fixed Assets

The way to calculate fixed assets is as follows: get your financial statements for at least the last three years. For each year, calculate the amount of fixed assets found on the balance sheet at the beginning and end of the period and divide by two. This gives you the average fixed asset value for each period.

$$\text{Average Fixed Assets} = \frac{(bFA + eFA)}{2}$$

(bFA = beginning fixed assets)
(eFA = ending fixed assets)

Then, calculate this ratio using the average fixed assets and net profit for each year.

$$\frac{\text{Net Profit}}{\text{Average Fixed Assets}}$$

If you find the fixed asset ratio is on the decline, it indicates that you have been investing more in fixed assets rather than in assets that produce an income. These fixed assets could be buildings, office equipment, vehicles, etc.—all the things that do not directly contribute to producing an income. There could be a logical and plausible reason for this, which is fine. If not, then this would be something which you need to be aware of and resolve where appropriate.

Remember, in business, your aim is to generate the most amount of cash flow, profit and sales, using as few assets as possible, thus giving you the greatest return. From there, you can make an informed decision as to which assets to purchase and when, in order to grow the business as quickly and efficiently as possible.

Profit Control

$$\frac{\text{COGS}}{\text{SALES}} \quad \& \quad \frac{\text{EXPENSES}}{\text{SALES}}$$

Another key element to being a successful business person is the ability to generate as much profit as possible. The quickest and easiest way to do this is by controlling the cost of goods sold (COGS) and expenses.

As touched upon already (and something we'll discuss in detail in the coming chapters), there is no point ramping up sales when you have no control over what you are spending. Doing so will simply make you a busy fool!

For profit control, if the ratios of COGS to sales and/or expenses to sales is increasing, it could reveal issues such as: the cost of goods you are buying is increasing; the sales team are discounting too much; or there has been too much spending on overheads. The aim is to get these numbers as low as possible and have a stable or downwards trend.

Cash Control

$$\frac{OCF}{PROFIT}$$

With any business, operating cash flow (OCF) is the lifeblood of its survival. Using this key measurement—OCF against profit—will show you how effective your business is at converting profit into cash. You want this number to be as high as possible.

Four Important Rules

1. OCF must be positive.

2. OCF must be greater than net profit.

3. OCF must be greater than fixed assets.

4. OCF must be trending in the same direction as net profit.

Knowing the numbers for these ratio calculations—return on sales (ROS), asset turnover, return on assets (ROA), profit control and cash control—is the first step to gaining and maintaining control of your business. These calculations need to be done on a monthly or quarterly basis. Anything longer than that will not give you enough data to signal any changes that may be happening within your business.

By carrying out these calculations regularly, we can join up the points and start creating trends. The more points along the trend-line, the more accurate it will be. This will enable you to very quickly see which trends are moving in the wrong direction and allow you to take corrective action before it becomes a more fundamental problem.

Maintaining full business optics enables you to spot potential problems when they first occur, enabling you to fix any issues straightaway. In order to have full business optics, it is advisable to measure these ratios regularly—monthly or at least quarterly. Remember, the aim is to look at the trends over time.

In this chapter we have examined the ratios that can be calculated using all three financial statements discussed in chapter 3. The ratios bring these three statements together and allow you to get a full picture of how your company is performing. Using these ratios, along with the information given in all three financial statements, will provide you with the necessary business optics to remain in control of your company and make key decisions based on real information.

In the next chapter, we examine the difference between profit and cash flow. We unpack the four cash flow zones and then dive into the six keys that make up the Cash Flow Code. We consider the importance of having a robust credit control system, negotiating with suppliers and keeping control of stock. We then look at two example companies to see the powerful effect expenses can have on your bottom line and bank account. By the end of the chapter, you will be fully armed to take back control of your cash flow!

Quick-Fire Actions

- Get three years' worth of management accounts and calculate your company's performance ratios.

- Check the performance of other companies in your industry.

- Measure and track your company's future performance using these ratios.

6   UNDERSTANDING CASH FLOW

PROFIT AND CASH FLOW are not the same thing.

Remember Robert Kiyosaki's definition of an asset: "anything that puts money in your pocket."

Note here that he uses the word "money". This interpretation does not define an asset as "anything that puts profit in your pocket!"

One of the key indicators and important metrics is how effectively your business can turn profit into cash.

Cash flow is what matters to investors or someone looking to buy your business in the future. How and when cash flows through your bank account is as important as actual accounting profits. What this means is that cash flow is also an important measurement when looking at the health of a business.

Profit (theoretical cash) is important in that it will ultimately be turned into cash. There are good reasons why accounting profits are calculated in the way they are.

However, cash flow tells a much clearer story of fluctuations, financial trends and one-off events.

Operating cash flow (OCF) reflects how much cash is being generated from a company's products or services. Earnings before interest, tax, depreciation and amortization (EBITDA) is closely related to operating cash flow and is often used as a cash flow measure.

Types of Cash

Not all cash is the same. We have operating cash, investment cash and financial cash. Let's look at each of these.

Operating Cash

At times, you'll see slight variations to this language, such as "cash provided by or used for operating activities". Whatever the exact language, this category includes all the cash flow, in and out, that is related to the actual operations of a business. It includes the cash customers send in when they pay their bills. It includes the cash the company pays out in salaries, to vendors and to the landlord, along with all the other cash it must spend to keep the doors open and the business operating.

Investment Cash

This label can be confusing. In this context, investing activities refer to investments made by the company, not by its owners. A key subcategory here is cash spent on capital investments—that is the purchase of assets. If the company buys a truck or a machine, the cash it paid out shows up on this part of the statement. Conversely, if the company sells a truck or a machine (or any other asset), the cash it receives shows up here as well. This section also includes investment in acquisitions or financial securities—in short, anything that involves the buying or selling of company assets.

Financing Cash

Financing refers to both the borrowing and paying back of loans and the transactions between the company and its shareholders. So, if a company receives a loan, the proceeds show up in this category. If a company gets an equity investment from a shareholder, that also shows up here. Should the company pay off the principal on a loan, buy back its own stock or pay a dividend to its shareholders, those expenditures of cash also would appear in this category. Here again is some label confusion: if a shareholder invests further money in a company, the cash involved shows up under financing, not investing.

Cash Flow vs. Profit

Profit is theoretical/calculated cash that you have made.

Cash is the reality, the physical money in your bank account.

Let's use a river as an analogy to explain this...

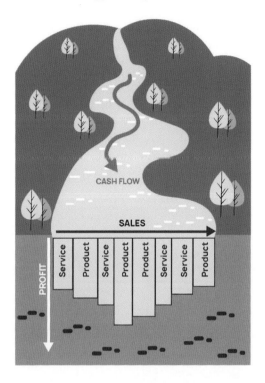

No matter which river we are talking about, every river will have a width, depth and current. All rivers will find the path of least resistance.

A business is exactly the same. Every business has sales—represented here by the width of the river. Every business makes an amount of profit—the more profit, the deeper the river. And every business must have a cash flow—the current or speed at which the river is flowing.

Warning: if a river has no water, it is no longer a river. In the same way, if a business has no cash flow, it is no longer a business.

We also need to be aware of any obstacles within the business that divert the flow of the river from its course (or cash away from our bank account). These come in the form of unnecessary expenditure, poor-performing assets or under-performing employees or anything that reduces the volume of water (cash) heading down river to your bank account.

As business owners, it is our goal to have a river that is as wide and deep as possible but also one that has a consistently strong current or cash flow.

The Four Zones of Cash Flow

Another way of looking at your company's health is to plot where you think your business is on the profit/cash flow zones as given in this graph:

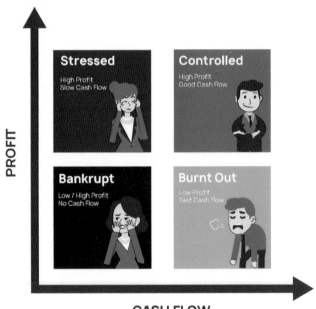

Bankrupt—swamp: little to no cash flow

Stressed—slow-moving river: sluggish cash flow

Burnt-Out—rapids: turbulent cash flow, shallow profits

Controlled—Healthy River: Efficient & Effective Cash Flow

Every business will fit into one of the four zones and almost every business will spend a period of time in each zone at some point during its life, or even during a yearly financial cycle.

The majority of businesses spend most of their time either in the stressed or burnt-out zones. In this chapter, I will be revealing to you my Cash Flow Code: the six key principles that will enable you to reduce the amount of time you spend in the three danger zones and increase your time in the controlled zone. But first, let us take a look at each zone in turn.

Bankrupt Zone—Swamp: Little to No Cash Flow

This is typically the graveyard zone. A business can only survive here for an extremely short period of time and they must have a clever plan of how to get out quickly. A business cannot survive for very long if cash flow is slow to non-existent, despite how good or bad the profits are.

Stressed Zone—Slow-Moving River: Sluggish Cash Flow

These are profitable businesses, but these are companies that have significant cash gaps—the gap or period of time between paying bills and receiving money from sales invoices. This is not necessarily a problem, provided the business has made provisions and has enough cash in the bank to bridge these gaps.

If cash runs out, companies will quickly move from the stressed zone to the bankrupt zone.

If profits fall, companies will then be moving towards the burnt-out zone.

Typical industries found in this zone are within the construction and automotive industries.

Burnt Out-Zone—Rapids: Turbulent Cash Flow, Shallow Profits

This is the business that feels they are constantly on a rapid treadmill—running fast but getting nowhere. They are fighting to keep their head above water and always chasing the next sale to get money in the bank. The business owner feels like they are on a hamster wheel, forever racing around trying to fill the ever-present cash gap. If sales start to slow down or expenses rise, this will ultimately push them into the bankrupt zone.

Typical industries in this zone include owner-run businesses and retailers who have business-to-business (B2B) sales. These businesses typically struggle to invoice and get paid on time.

Controlled Zone—Healthy River: Efficient & Effective Cash Flow

The controlled zone is the sweet spot: the ultimate goal of any business. Cash flow and profit are both good and there is balance within the company. There are systems and processes in place to grow the business and to protect cash flow.

Cash Flow Code

Using the Cash Flow Code principles, you can move a business out of either the stressed or burnt-out zones and into the controlled zone. If you can move quickly enough, have the correct product/service and have a good team around you, you could even move a business currently in the bankrupt zone into the controlled zone.

However, there is a warning: each business owner will need to get the correct code sequence; otherwise, it could make the situation worse.

As explained in chapter 1, my retail business that I started when I was in my 20s was in the burnt-out zone. I urgently needed more money, so the most obvious route to take was to increase sales and marketing. The theory seemed sound: get more sales, make more profit and that would solve my problem...**WRONG...!**

As you will soon see, in order to get the most out of this strategy, there is a sequence you must follow. There are six keys that you must follow in their given sequence. I will take you through these six keys, explaining each in turn so that you can then apply them to your own business.

The sequence fits into two categories: cash flow and profit. As cash flow is the life-blood of a business, we need to address this area first. There is little point in maximising profits when we cannot convert profits into cash in the bank. Once we have fixed the cash flow, we can then focus on maximising profits. This will not only increase the bank balance but should ultimately make the business more profitable. So, we start by looking at the first three keys that will maximise cash flow.

The Code

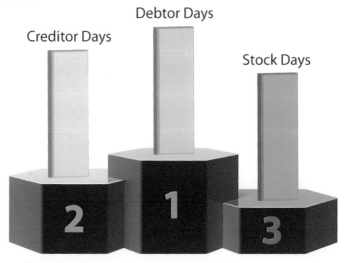

Maximising Cash Flow

There are three keys to maximising cash flow:

1. The first key is to reduce the number of days it takes for you to get paid.

2. The second is to increase the number of days before paying suppliers.

   ** WARNING ** There is a big caution here—avoid causing ill feeling between you and your suppliers. You do not want to become a bad customer for your suppliers. I will explain this in more detail under the Increase Creditor Days section.

3. The third is to decrease the amount of stock days, thus freeing up cash that can be spent on faster-moving stock.

Let us now look at each of these keys individually.

Key 1: Reduce Debtor Days

Debtor days is the average number of days it takes from the date of invoice to the day you have that invoice paid. Debtor days can be calculated using the amount found in the balance sheet under *accounts receivable*.

Formula: Debtor Days = Account Receivables ÷ (Sales ÷ days in year or days in month)

Debtor days is a big key and one that I come across most often when consulting. The aim here is to reduce the number of days between invoicing for goods sold or services rendered and physically getting paid. Here are some tips that I have found effective in reducing debtor days in my companies:

- Reduce your payment terms from 30 days to 14 days.
- Run collections on a weekly basis.
- Have a credit-control process in place:
  - Confirm receipt of the invoice.
  - Ensure the client has no queries on the invoice.
  - Contact each client seven days before payment is due.
  - Chase on the day of payment, if not received.
  - Confirm payment when received.
  - Thank the client for the payment.
- Play good cop/bad cop. Use a third party or another member of staff to chase invoices, allowing you to preserve your relationship with the client.
- For each client, find out:
  - Whom to direct the invoice to
  - What their payment process is
- Invoice immediately.
- When carrying out collections: be firm, friendly and focused.
- Have an answer/solution for every reason why a client will not/cannot pay you:
  - Oversight: agree on a payment date.
  - Unable to pay: agree on a payment plan.

- Got a query: resolve the issue.
- Won't pay: take action.

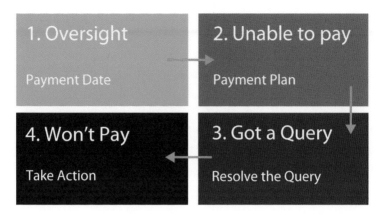

In dealing with these four scenarios over the years, I have created and tested many email and letter templates, as well as telephone scripts. I have compiled the very best templates that I know work into a single document that can be downloaded and implemented straightaway. In this document, I have explained exactly how and when to use the various templates in order to get paid whilst, more crucially, preserving relationships with your customers. To get your copy, please visit www.businessoptics.co.uk/resources.

Quick-Fire Actions

- Set customer expectations.
- Enforce payment terms.
- Be proactive—He who makes the most noise ...
- Incentivise your customers to pay on time.
- Get a credit card payment backup.*
- Keep A & B Clients and get rid of C & D Customers.**

*Credit Card Payment Backup

As a rule of thumb, always make it as easy as possible for people to buy from you and to PAY YOU! All too often, I have heard clients say, "The cheque is in the post" or "It is on this week's pay run", to find that nothing materialises. As far as possible, have a way for a client to make a payment over the phone. Nowadays, there are many apps and services available that make this possible.

**A-B-C-D Clients

The 80/20 rule states that 80% of a company's profits come from just 20% of its customer base. It makes good business sense to offer excellent customer service to all your clients; however, not all clients are equal. All too often, key business resources are spent dealing with clients that contribute very little to overall sales and profit, leaving the business less time to deal with the clients who are most valuable to the company.

Understanding how customers impact your business is critical for the following reasons:

1. If you are looking to grow your business, do not focus additional resources on demanding and unprofitable customers.

2. A higher level of service could be offered to your existing, more profitable customers.

3. Understanding the type of client you want will create a more targeted marketing strategy and reduce client acquisition costs.

4. Improve profit margins by getting rid of expensive, non-profit-making clients.

5. Improve staff morale: demanding customers tend to be those who complain more and are usually more demanding to work with. They have the potential to be awkward and often do not value what you do.

Customer Analysis

Make a list of all your existing and potential customers, broken down into categories based on turnover, then profitability:

- High Turnover: high, medium, low profitability
- Medium Turnover: high, medium, low profitability
- Low Turnover: high, medium, low profitability

You should now have three lists that you can rank as A, B, C or D.

To help you rank your clients in this way, you can download my free client-assessment tool from www.businessoptics.co.uk/resources.

Here's how to rank your clients:

A-Grade Client	The people who you love working with and who get you up in the morning. They pay well and refer you on to other clients, who then bring you more business. These clients really like what you deliver and they come back to you repeatedly, becoming a "raving fan" of your business. Your team provides them with excellent service.
B-Grade Client	They are not quite raving fans, but they still provide a significant contribution to your business. They are on the verge of becoming an A-Grade client. Your team gives your D-Grade clients a fairly good amount of attention. These clients are happy with your service and they represent a healthy volume of sales.
C-Grade Client	This client is lukewarm. You need to decide whether they are worth nurturing into a B-Grade client or downgrade them to a D-Grade client. They might be a client that you could work with in small doses, but you will need to monitor them to see if they contribute to the company's overall sales and profit.
D-Grade Client	A D-Grade client could mean that you have tried to work with them in the past, but it's just not working out. They do not pay on time, they have too many complaints (often unsubstantiated) and they are a drain on your company's time and resources. The best thing is to hand them over to your competitors, so you can concentrate on your A-B-C clients.

When you examine your client list and the number of A, B, C and D clients you have, you may find you have a small number of A's. If so, look at your business as a whole and find out why that is happening. The aim is to develop as many as you can and the key is to never have a client who contributes more than 10% of your annual turnover. If a client is responsible for more than 10% of your annual turnover, this could leave your business vulnerable should that client leave or stop trading. Always try to spread the risk and avoid a single point of failure. By increasing your number of A-Grade clients, you will spread the highest percentage of turnover across a higher number of good customers.

With a clear understanding of how much value each client gives your business, you can work with those viable groups to up-sell, cross-sell and diversify products and services across your customer base. It is far easier, cheaper and faster to sell more products or services to people who already know you than to find new customers who have never bought from you. Applying this strategy will provide your business with long-term stability and increased profits.

Now that we have explored how to reduce debtor days whilst maintaining good customer relations, we can explore the second key of the Cash Flow Code: increase creditor days.

Key 2: Increase Creditor Days

Creditor days or *accounts payable* (found on the Balance Sheet) is the average time it takes a business to settle its debts with trade suppliers.

Formula: Creditor Days = Accounts Payable ÷ ((COS + Total Expenses) ÷ days in year or days in month)

The ratio is a useful indicator when it comes to assessing the liquidity position of a business, in other words to determine if the company has sufficient cash flow to pay its immediate debts.

The creditor days figure is a similar ratio to debtor days. It gives an insight into whether a business is taking full advantage of the trade credit available to it.

Uncharacteristically high creditor days, meaning a company takes a long time to pay a supplier, can indicate cash flow problems within a business.

Conversely, low creditor days, meaning a company is paying suppliers too quickly, can show that a business may not be maximising available credit terms, thus not managing their cash flow to its full potential.

Tip #1 Calculate creditor days to give a true reflection of cash flow.

Be aware that, sometimes, creditor days are calculated only using cost of goods sold (COGS). From a cash flow perspective, this is not accurate enough.

In order to calculate the impact that creditor days has on cash flow, we need to include COGS plus expenses and overheads. This will give us the total cash leaving the bank account on a monthly basis. After all, in order for the business to run, it needs to pay more than the COGS. For instance, you must take into account the monthly cost of rent, advertising, marketing, professional fees, vehicles, staff costs, office administration, etc., which fall under expenses and overheads.

If a company only uses the COGS in the calculation, this results in a skewed number of creditor days.

Tip #2 Negotiate credit terms with suppliers.

In general, a business that wants to maximise its cash flow should take as long as possible to pay its bills. However, there are obvious risks associated with taking more time than is permitted by the terms of trade with the supplier, from the loss of supplier goodwill to the potential threat of legal action or late-payment charges.

You can also argue that it is ethical to pay suppliers on time, particularly if your suppliers are small and rely on timely payments of their invoices in order to manage their own cash flow.

What I do in these situations is go to each of my suppliers and say to them something like this:

> "Dear Supplier, I spend £X (or $X) with you each year. I always pay my account on time and you never have to chase me for payment. I am looking to grow my business by X% this year, which will increase my monthly/yearly spend with you. If I were to increase my spend with your company, could you offer me some discount or economies of scale?"

If the answer is no, my next question is:

> "Dear Supplier, I totally understand and appreciate we are in business and we both need to make a profit. If you are

unable to offer any further discount or economies of scale, could you extend my credit terms by a further 30 days?"

I always go in higher with a view of us agreeing to a possible 15-day extension or at worst an extra 5 days. Any extension you manage to get will be a bonus to you and you can see the impact this will have when you run your business through the Cash Flow Simulator at www.businessoptics.co.uk.

For more information about credit days and extra tips, please visit www.businessoptics.co.uk.

Quick-Fire Actions

- Never pay suppliers late.
- Do not pay invoices early.
- Try to negotiate longer payment terms.
- Avoid late payment charges.

Having considered debtor days and creditor days, we can now turn to the third key of the Cash Flow Code—decreasing stock days.

Key 3: Decrease Stock Days

Stock days (or inventory days) are the average number of days that goods remain in stock before being sold. As a measure of short-term sales potential, a number above the industry norm indicates problems with sales forecasts. Conversely, a number below the norm indicates loss of sales due to the company's inability to fulfil demand. Stock days are also called days cover, stock cover, days of stock or day's sales to stock.

Formula: Average Stock ÷ Sales x 365

The stock days calculation measures the number of days it will take a company to sell all of its stock. In other words, the stock days ratio shows how many days a company's current stock supply will last.

This is important to both creditors and investors for three main reasons. It measures value, liquidity and cash flow. Investors and creditors want to know how valuable a company's stock is. Older, more obsolete stock is always worth less than current, fresh stock. The day's sales in stock shows how fast the company is moving its goods. In other words, it shows how fresh the stock is.

This calculation also shows the liquidity of stock. Shorter stock days means the company can convert its stock into cash sooner, i.e., the stock is extremely liquid. The more liquid the stock, the better the cash flow.

Ending stock is found on the balance sheet and the cost of goods sold is listed on the income statement. Note that you can calculate the days in stock for any period; all you need to do is adjust the multiple.

What are the reasons for high stock days?

Stock days are high when the stock turnover is low. Since stock turnover is associated with sales and average stock held, changes in either sales or stock can cause a high amount of stock days. For example, if a company's sales have dropped, this will cause the stock days to increase.

But how many days of stock should I carry?

This will all depend on:
- whether your company has enough money to pay for all of the stock
- how long it takes to replenish your stock

When it comes to understanding how much stock you should carry, understanding your supplier lead times is one of the most important factors. For example, if you have ten days of stock, but it takes your supplier 21 days to resupply you, then you may have a gap in customer delivery.

You may order more stock from your supplier today, but if it takes them 21 days to deliver that stock to you, you are going to run out of stock in ten days, so you would have 11 days when you are unable to fulfil customer demand.

How do I carry zero days of stock and still stay in business?

If you are able to carry zero days of stock, which means that you haven't spent any money upfront for stock, this is a great result!

But you still need to sell products to be a viable company. So here are some tips:

1. Work with your suppliers to drive their lead times down.

2. Manage your customers' expectations so that they place orders with a lead time that aligns with your suppliers' lead times.

3. Once you receive an order from your customer, place an order with your supplier.

For example:

- Your supplier can supply you in three days.
- Your customer knows that you'll ship their order four days after they place it with you.
- Your customer places their order and you order from your supplier.
- Your supplier's order arrives in three days.
- It takes you one day to receive, process and prepare the customer order.
- You ship your customer their order on the fourth day.

This way, everyone wins.

Remember, stock days is a unit of measure that helps drive optimised stock management. By understanding it, you can manage stock levels and reorder points, as well as reduce stock shortages— all of which allows you greater cash flow.

Quick-Fire Actions

- If possible, place smaller stock orders.
- Negotiate delivery terms and fees.
- Sell all old and slow-moving stock.

- Track what sells and what doesn't.
- Do not let suppliers unilaterally stock your shelves.
- Monitor stock loss—stealing, etc.

Now that we have explored the first three keys of the Cash Flow Code, related to maximising cash flow, we can turn our attention to keys 4, 5 and 6, which deal with simple, systematic approaches to maximise profits and ultimately increase cash flow even more.

Maximising Profits

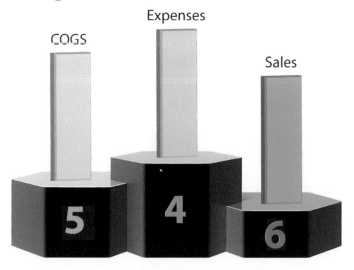

When looking for ways to increase or maximise profits, the most obvious and often the most logical thing to do is to increase sales. I hope that, by now, you will realise that there is a far easier way to increase profits and I will show you how.

Rule 1: Always pick the low-hanging fruit first.

Rule 2: You must work hard by first working smarter.

Rule 3: Repeat rule 1 and rule 2.

Key 4: Reduce Expenses

The quickest and easiest way to maximise profits is to first reduce expenses. Let me explain this using an example:

There are two companies ABC Ltd and XYZ Ltd.

They both made sales of £1,000 for the year, with a net profit of £100. At the start of the financial year, their goal is to increase profits by 30%.

Both companies look like this:

	ABC Ltd	XYZ Ltd	%
Sales	£1,000.00	£1,000.00	0%
Expenses	£ 900.00	£ 900.00	90%
Profit	£ 100.00	£ 100.00	10%

By the end of the year, both companies hit their goal of making 30% more profit, i.e., from £100.00 to £130.00, but each went about it very differently. Let's see what each did:

ABC Ltd		%
Sales	£1,200.00	20%
Expenses	£1,070.00	89%
Profit	£ 130.00	11%

Assuming company ABC Ltd made a saving of 1% through economies of scale, they have achieved a 30% increase in profits by increasing sales by 20%.

However, company XYZ Ltd's sales remained exactly the same, but they too increased profits by 30%. This is what they did:

XYZ Ltd		%
Sales	£1,000.00	0%
Expenses	£ 870.00	87%
Profit	£ 130.00	13%

The only activity XYZ Ltd undertook was to cut their expenses by 3%, which made them an extra £30 profit for the year.

Looking at the above examples, which one would be easiest to achieve—cutting expenses by 3% or increasing sales by 20%?

Company XYZ Ltd can now increase sales by 20% and we will directly compare both companies:

	ABC Ltd	XYZ Ltd
Sales	£1,200.00	£1,200.00
Expenses	£1,070.00	£1031.00
Profit	£ 130.00	£ 169.00

As you can see, XYZ Ltd enabled themselves to produce an extra £39.00 profit—23% more than company ABC Ltd—simply by first finding a 3% saving in expenses.

This is how, if you work smarter at the start by first cutting expenses, when you increase sales later on, you can achieve a lot more with the same amount of effort.

It is not uncommon for a business to be over-spending by around 10% on items that play no part in producing an income. I am very confident that I would be able to walk into any business and find at least 5% worth of savings within the first 30 days. As a matter of fact, I urge you to take me up on this challenge with your business: you can email me at hello@businessoptics.co.uk or find me at www.businessoptics.co.uk.

Having examined your company's expenses and identified the areas where savings could be made, we can then look at the fifth key— reducing the cost of goods sold.

Key 5: Reduce Cost of Goods Sold (COGS)

Gross margin is what remains from sales after you have covered your direct product or service costs. Gross margin is measured and expressed as a percentage of sales to help demonstrate how much is left over to pay for the running of the business.

It is good practice to contact your suppliers at least once a year, as well as to search around for any new suppliers out there who would be hungry for your business.

When contacting suppliers, it is good to have on hand the amount spent with each supplier over the past 12 months. Use that as leverage and explain that you are looking to grow your business, which will, therefore, increase your spend with them. Also remind them that you pay your bills on time. Be upfront and ask for better rates.

Please note that just as you should not rely on one client for more than 10% of your total sales, no one supplier should account for more than 10% of your total spend. In the same way, this could make your business vulnerable should that supplier cease trading, change product ranges or increase prices.

By using the Cash Flow Simulator Tool found at www.businessoptics.co.uk, you will be able to see the impact that reducing COGS will have on both the profit and cash flow in your business. Monitoring COGS over time will highlight any price increases, which will allow you to either increase the sales price or look to reduce these costs by changing suppliers or find efficiencies if you are a service base business. Unlike most business owners, who only find this out months later after the year-end, by which time the damage is done and will take a lot longer to rectify, you will have greater control over what is going on with your cash flow and the profits of your company in real time.

Now that we have our house in order, we can finally turn our attention to the company's sales. Following keys 1 to 5 first will dramatically increase the impact of the sixth and final key—increasing sales.

Key 6: Increase Sales

You have now implemented robust credit control systems, which are in place and working. You have negotiated payment terms with suppliers and streamlined your stock to sort out any cash flow problems.

You have looked at all business-related expenses and cost of sales to maximise profits, making the company as efficient and effective as possible. Now is the time when you can press the "sales and marketing" button and benefit from building a solid foundation for success.

As can be seen in the previous example, this will not only have a dramatic effect on profits but on your cash flow as well.

How to Increase Sales

The key to growing your business is to look after your existing customer base BEFORE looking to get new customers.

Take your business partner or sales team and explore all the products or services you offer. Be creative and look for ways you can bundle, add and create packages with your existing products or services. The aim here is to create value for your customers in such a way that price doesn't matter anymore and they would not bother to look elsewhere.

The strategic part is to not compete on price but on value. The value is what you are offering to your customers by way of products or services. Can you offer something a competitor cannot? Can you add complementary products or services that your customers would value more than if they were simply standalone items? By doing so, the more perceived value you can add, the less focused the customer will be on price.

There are three parts to increasing sales.

1. Internal

- Firstly, confirm whether your existing customers know about all the products or services you offer. The chances are that they only know a fraction of what you offer so, by strategically marketing to your current client base, you can educate them in all that you have to offer. It is much easier to cross-sell or up-sell to an existing client than to a cold customer.

- Ask for testimonials, especially video testimonials. This can be used for both internal and external marketing and is a great way of engaging with clients.

- Meet up with your customers to ask each client what they think of your product or service (or find an external company to carry this out for you). If any area needs improving, ensure it is dealt with and rectified.

- Ask each client whether they know of someone who could benefit from your product or service, incentivizing them with an attractive offer for both themselves and their referral. A warm lead or referral will dramatically cut your client acquisition cost.

2. External

- This includes all digital marketing.
- Optimise your website.
- Create up-sells, cross-sells and down-sells.
- Use email sequencing, etc.

3. Mergers and Acquisitions

- The quickest and easiest way to double or even quadruple the size of your business within 18 months is to buy a competitor, supplier or even a customer who is also a business-to-business (B2B) customer.

In summary, we first looked at the difference between profit and cash flow and explored the different types of cash used within a business. We addressed the four cash flow zones and then, using the numbers on a balance sheet and P&L statements, focused on the six keys that directly and indirectly affect cash flow to make the business as profitable and cash-rich as possible, before increasing sales (which is the final key, number 6).

In the next chapter, I will introduce you to the Cash Flow Simulator. Before undertaking any substantial changes to the company, such as increasing sales or taking on a large new client that will only pay invoices in 90 days instead of your 30-day terms, it is wise to double-check what impact this will have on your business, especially in terms of cash flow. The Cash Flow Simulator will provide you with the optics required to make those key decisions.

Quick-Fire Actions

- Determine which cash flow zone your business is operating in.

- Implement the six keys to improving cash flow and increasing profits.

- Run the Cash Flow Simulator Tool and find out how your six keys are working. Simply go to www.businessoptics.co.uk.

7   THE CASH FLOW SIMULATOR

AS A BUSINESS OWNER, you want the hard work you put into your company to give you the biggest possible return. After all, who would want to increase profits by £10,000.00 when, with the same amount of effort, you could increase them by £40,000.00?

At the same time, you do not want to work hard to increase your profits, only to find you actually have no money in the bank!

I appreciate it would seem counterintuitive to ignore increasing sales first and to rather focus on the other five keys instead—debtor days, creditor days, stock days, expenses and COGS.

To understand why it is so effective to hold off increasing sales until after you've focused on the other five keys, let's compare it to driving up a steep, snowy mountain road. The pressing goal is to reach the mountain top and, as such, the temptation is to simply get in your car—even though it is equipped with summer tyres—and go, go, go. This approach is akin to increasing sales in order to increase profits.

However, by simply pausing for an hour to attach snow chains, check the fuel level and de-ice the windscreen, the drive up the icy mountain pass will be a lot safer, quicker and more enjoyable. This second approach is the equivalent of primarily focusing on the other five keys and, only after these are addressed, look to increase sales, which will ultimately reap the greatest increase in profit and cash flow.

Of course, I understand that for a lot of us, simply getting up the mountain (increasing sales) is the goal and the temptation to jump in the car and drive is very real and ever present. Even still, I urge you to pause for a while and ensure everything in your business is running efficiently and smoothly before increasing sales. This will give you the very best chance of success and a better return for all your efforts.

In the simulation below, I will show you the results of increasing sales first as opposed to addressing the other keys first and leaving sales as the final element. After considering the results, you can decide for yourself which route you would prefer to take.

Cash Flow Simulator

Based upon the previous 12 months' metrics and by simulating any changes you plan on making to your business, the Cash Flow Simulator enables you to forecast your profit and cash flow for the next 12 months. This allows you to test what will make the biggest impact to your business before actually taking action, enabling you to plan strategically for your company's development and growth.

Being able to plan and make informed decisions in this way allows you to maintain control over the business, preventing you from making the same mistake I made, which I will share with you a bit later in this chapter.

Using the Cash Flow Simulator

To begin using the simulator, you will need to input the seven key numbers achieved in the previous 12 months. These numbers, which can be found in your company's balance sheet, P&L statement and cash flow statement, are:

- Sales
- Cost of Sales
- Expenses
- Accounts Receivable or Debtor Days
- Accounts Payable or Creditor Days
- Inventory/Stock or Stock Days
- Cash in the Bank at the Start of the Period

The Simulator's Two Sections

The Simulator is divided into two sections:

- Balance Sheet—the three keys that directly affect cash flow
- Profit & Loss—the three keys that indirectly affect cash flow

Balance Sheet Account

The top three keys that directly affect cash flow can be found on your company's balance sheet.

Accounts Receivable: this will be calculated in terms of debtor days. As previously mentioned, a debtor day is the length of time it takes your customers to pay you from the date you issued the invoice. You will want this number to be as small as possible.

Accounts Payable: this will be calculated in terms of creditor days. Also mentioned already, a creditor day is the length of time it takes you to pay your supplier from the date you receive their invoice. You will want this number to be as high as possible *BUT a word of warning here:* you must never be a bad customer to your supplier. The best way of increasing the length of time to pay your suppliers is to call them and renegotiate credit terms, as outlined already in chapter 6.

Inventory/Stock: this will be calculated in terms of stock days. Stock days, as defined earlier, are the amount of days it will take you to sell all your stock. You will want this number to be as small as possible for your industry, which means the stock you have is fast-moving and there is no dead money sitting on your shelves.

If your business is more of a service-based business, you may not have any stock. That is absolutely fine; just leave that field blank.

Profit & Loss Account

When the simulator has been loaded with your company's previous 12 months' data, you will be able to see how any changes to your sales will affect your profits and, more importantly, cash flow. The Cash Flow Simulator affords you the opportunity to see if you can fine-tune your business to gain the maximum return for an increase in revenue.

The areas in your profit and loss account that will dramatically affect profits will be your cost of sales and expenses. If any of these figures can be reduced, even by 1%, this will have a big impact on how well your business performs.

Simulator Results

The results of any changes you make to sales, cost of sales, expenses, debtor days, creditor days and stock days will be shown on the right-hand side of the Cash Flow Simulator, in both table and graph form.

The Cash Flow Simulator allows you to play with these numbers and shows you the result—be it positive or negative—of what will happen if you were to implement those changes to your business. It gives you a chance to see which changes will be most effective for increasing cash flow and, ultimately, how efficient you can make your business.

The saying, "Turnover is vanity, profit is sanity, BUT cash is REALITY", is very true. Therefore, I recommend the order in which you make these changes is firstly to your balance sheet, then to your profit and loss account. Fix any cash leaks first; then look to drive the business forward.

A Real-Life Example

In this book's first chapter, I shared my experience of running a profitable retail business that was on a cash flow rollercoaster. As my business was profitable, it only seemed logical to me that the way to gain control and security and stop the rollercoaster was to increase sales. This logic stands to reason because, if you know you are profitable, all you need to do is sell more at the same or a higher margin to increase profits.

So, we implemented an ambitious marketing campaign, targeting both retail and commercial customers. Our biggest increase in sales came from the commercial side: it accounted for around 95% of the 20% overall increase in sales.

Needless to say, we were over the moon! It was no mean feat growing a business by 20% in only a few short months. However, after all the extra man-hours and stress invested into securing such an increase in sales, we actually had less cash in the bank. We were worse off than before! Instead of getting us off the rollercoaster, our rollercoaster simply became a wilder ride. A part of me wished we had never embarked on the growth exercise.

I was perplexed by this situation and it took me a while to figure out what was really going on inside the business. After all, my knowledge of business up to that point was very simplistic: *you buy a product for £1, sell it for £2, pay £0.50 for expenses and you are left with £0.50 profit.* Theoretically, that is exactly how a business operates in its most simplistic form.

So what happened to enable my business to grow by 20%, yet leave us with less money in the bank?

Let me use the Cash Flow Simulator to show you.

To begin, you will need to load the simulator—www.businessoptics.co.uk—with the seven key figures found in the company balance sheet, profit and loss statement and cash flow statement, which are the following:

Balance Sheet
- Accounts Receivable or Debtor Days
- Accounts Payable or Creditor Days
- Stock/Inventory or Stock Days

Profit & Loss
- Sales
- Cost of Sales (COGS)
- Expenses

Cash Flow Statement
- Cash in the Bank at the Start of the Period

Load the Simulator

The figures for my business were as follows:

Sales	£ 248,672.00
Cost of Sales (COGS)	£ 149,203.00
Expenses	£ 79,575.00
Accounts Receivable	£ 32,702.00
Accounts Payable	£ 17,550.00
Stock / Inventory	£ 25,753.00
Cash in the bank	£ 4,863.00

At this point, you can either enter the amount in accounts receivables or, if you know the debtor days, you can enter that figure. The same applies for accounts payable and stock/inventory.

The simulator will automatically calculate the debtor days, creditor days and stock days for you.

Profit & Loss Controls

Sales / Turnover: *Please provide the total sales / turnover for the past 12 months*	248672
Cost of Sales: *Please provide the total cost of sales for the past 12 months*	149203
Total Expenses: *Please provide the total expenses for the past 12 months*	79575
EBITDA (Click update to calculate)	19894

Balance Sheet Controls

Accounts Receivable: *Please provide the amount for accounts receivable*	20439
OR	
Debtor Days: *If you know your debtor days please insert them here*	30
Accounts Payable: *Please provide the amount for accounts payable*	12536
OR	
Creditor Days: *If you know your creditor days please insert them here*	20
Stock / Inventory: *Please provide the current amount of stock being held*	25753
OR	
Stock Days: *If you know your stock days please insert them here*	63

Cash Flow Statement

Cash: *Please provide the cash balance in your account*	4863

If you chose to input figures into both cells (the monetary amount and days), the simulator will use the accounts receivables, accounts payables and stock/inventory amounts to calculate the days. Therefore, if you wish to calculate the monetary value of accounts receivables, accounts payables and stock/inventory, please ensure the amounts are left blank with only the days inputted.

Once these figures are entered, you can click the "Update" button.

UPDATE

The simulator will then calculate your EBITDA (earnings before interest, tax, depreciation and amortization) and either your debtor days, creditor days and stock days; or accounts receivables, accounts payable and stock/inventory.

You can now either click the "Run the Simulator" tab or "Run the Simulator" button.

RUN THE SIMULATOR

RUN THE SIMULATOR

Run the Simulator

If you inputted the numbers I gave you for my retail business, you will now see how my business had been performing for the last 12 months. Also, you'll see how if I did absolutely nothing, there would be no change to the business. Obviously this is not an option. If your business is not constantly changing or adapting, it will not progress and, in this competitive market place, you cannot afford to rest on your laurels—you will simply lose ground.

Simulation Results

	Past 12 Months	Projected 12 Months	Difference
Sales	248,672	248,672	0
Profit (EBITDA)	19,894	19,894	0
Operating Cash Flow	4,863	4,863	0

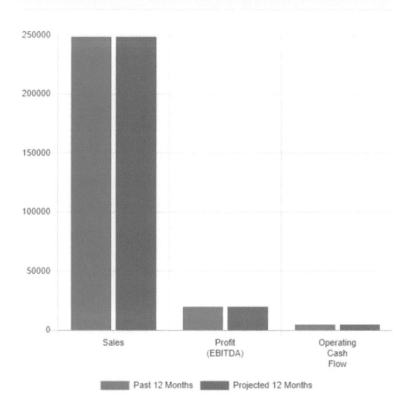

However, as already explained, in my attempt at escaping the cash flow rollercoaster I was on, I increased sales by 20% and this is what happened:

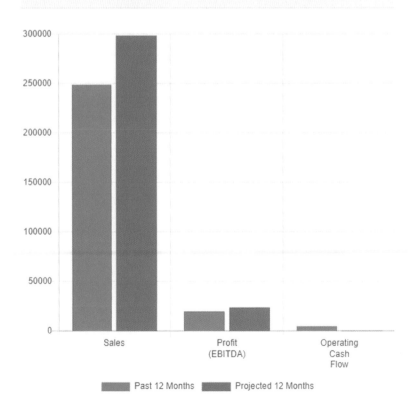

Simulation Results

	Past 12 Months	Projected 12 Months	Difference
Sales	248,672	298,406	49,734
Profit (EBITDA)	19,894	23,873	3,979
Operating Cash Flow	4,863	662	-4,201

My sales increased by £49,734.00 and profits went up by £3,978.00, all as expected. But, despite my increase in profits of £3,978.00, I was making a cash LOSS of £4,202.00!

That is what left me scratching my head all those years ago...

So, what happened and what should I have done differently?

A Look at the Cash Flow Code

Although sales is part of the Cash Flow Code, as you already learned in chapter 6, it is the last key you use—the last step in the process. To increase cash flow, I should have addressed the other five keys before increasing sales.

The first three keys I needed to address come from my balance sheet—accounts receivable, accounts payable and stock/inventory.

Balance Sheet Controls

Key Indicators	Days	Projected 12 Months	Past
Debtor Days	48	39,242	48
Creditor Days	28	21,060	28
Stock Days	63	30,903	63

Debtor Days

From the balance sheet controls you can see that my debtor days were 48 days. My payment terms clearly stated I was to be paid 30 days from the date of invoice. This told me I was only getting paid, on average, 48 days from when the invoice was first sent out (which is obviously beyond the 30 requested days). I clearly had a huge cash gap and I needed to implement a rigid credit control system.

This is what the newly implemented credit control system looked like:

- Changed payment terms from 30 days to 14 days.

- Chased each invoice two weeks, then one week, then the day before it was due. Then chased again on the day it was due.

- Created email templates, letter templates and telephone scripts for my staff to use to chase all outstanding invoices.

- Thanked the customer once payment was received.

Over the course of the next quarter, we managed to reduce the debtor days from 48 to 35.

These were the results: the simple act of implementing a comprehensive credit control system enabled me to increase my cash flow by a staggering £8,857.00!

Simulation Results

	Past 12 Months	Projected 12 Months	Difference
Sales	248,672	248,672	0
Profit (EBITDA)	19,894	19,894	0
Operating Cash Flow	4,863	13,720	8,857

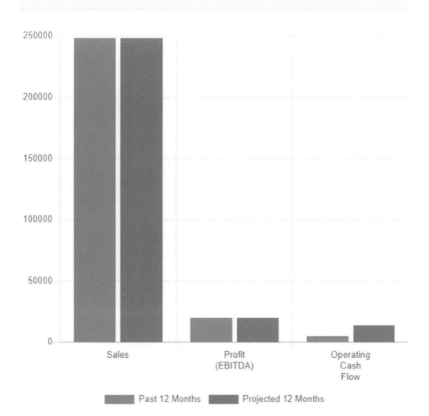

Creditor Days

Next, we looked at how quickly we paid our suppliers. I called them and re-negotiated payment terms. Some were receptive and some were not. However, we managed to increase our creditor days from an average of 28 to 31 days. This might not sound like much but the result was an extra £1,880.00 in cash flow, bringing the total added cash flow to £10,737.00.

Simulation Results

	Past 12 Months	Projected 12 Months	Difference
Sales	248,672	248,672	0
Profit (EBITDA)	19,894	19,894	0
Operating Cash Flow	4,863	15,600	10,737

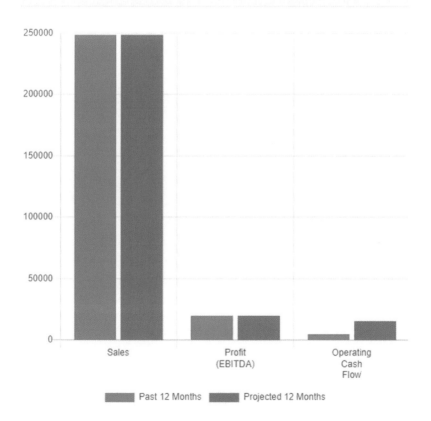

Stock Days

We then turned our focus to the amount of stock we were carrying. A list was made of all the slow-moving stock and stock that we held for a particular customer who needed that item delivered on the same day they placed the order.

We created a discount sale, whereby we sold all slow-moving stock, with some items being sold at cost price. Our aim was to get the money off the shelves and back into our bank account or reinvested into faster-moving stock.

For the customers who wanted us to keep stock for them, we implemented the following procedures:

- We informed the customer that their item now had a lead-time of two to four days.

- They could either purchase spare items to keep in THEIR stockroom, or we could hold the item for them but a pre-payment of 50% would be required to hold it.

- Alternatively, they needed to place the order with us two to four days before they required it.

From memory, I do not think any customers complained about these changes and most were actually thankful to us for informing them of the change in circumstances.

By carrying out this audit, we reduced our stock days from 63 to 44 days.

Reducing the stock days by 19 days resulted in a cash flow increase of £7,358.00, bringing the total added cash flow to £18,095.00—an incredible increase!

Simulation Results

	Past 12 Months	Projected 12 Months	Difference
Sales	248,672	248,672	0
Profit (EBITDA)	19,894	19,894	0
Operating Cash Flow	4,863	23,367	18,504

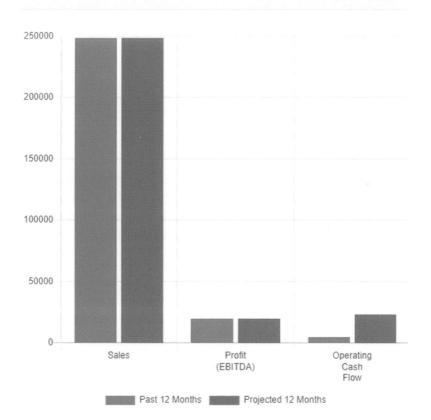

As you can see, by controlling the three balance sheet keys and focusing on the operational side of the business (as opposed to sales), we improved our cash position by a remarkable £18,095.00. This was simply retrieving our money, which was either sitting in our customers' bank accounts, suppliers' bank accounts or on our shelves.

This improvement required no extra man-hours, no extra stress and no extra overheads. It was simply managing the cash that we rightfully earnt and converting the profit into cash in the bank. As discussed previously, cash is the life-blood of a business. If you have no cash, you have no business. Therefore, it is crucial that these first three keys are controlled and managed correctly. Controlling these keys demonstrates that you have mastery over the operational processes within that part of your business; that you are not only in the driver's seat but fully aware of the inner-workings of the engine that will drive you forward.

The final three keys needing attention can be found in the profit and loss account—expenses, cost of sales (COGS) and finally sales.

Expenses

It is always advisable to review expenses every six months or at least once a year. This will enable you to keep the company running as efficiently as possible. By simply following the fourth rule in chapter 4 and being brutally honest with yourself, you should easily find 3% to 15% worth of savings.

As for my company, I managed to find 3% worth of savings very quickly. By finding a mere 3% worth of savings, my profit increased by £7,461.00 to £27,355.00 and my cash flow by £25,332.00 to £30,195.00, all by simply being a little more cautious about our spending!

Simulation Results

	Past 12 Months	Projected 12 Months	Difference
Sales	248,672	248,672	0
Profit (EBITDA)	19,894	27,355	7,461
Operating Cash Flow	4,863	30,195	25,332

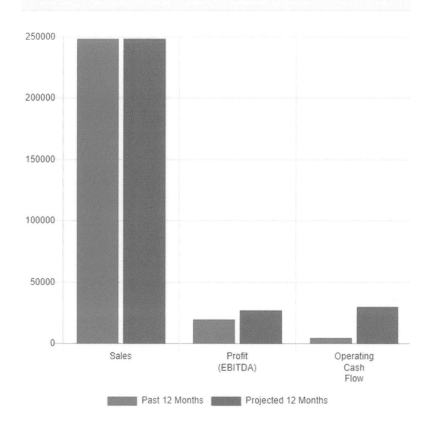

Cost of Sale/Cost of Goods Sold

As already discussed in the creditor days section of chapter 6, it is a worthwhile exercise, at least every six to 12 months, to look at how much you are spending with every supplier.

Ensuring that you pay your invoices on time and are armed with the yearly spend for that supplier, you will be in a good position to negotiate on price. Be ready to share with them what your future goals are, i.e., to grow your business and hence, increase your spend with them.

It is also advisable to shop around as another supplier may have started trading and be offering discounts or offers to any new customers.

The aim here is two-fold: to reduce your cost of goods sold and to increase or stretch payment terms WHILST, at the same time, ensuring good quality products or services.

At the time of carrying out this exercise I managed to find only a 2% saving. Let's see what those savings yielded: by reducing my cost of goods sold (COGS) from 60% to 58%, I achieved an increase in profits by £12,434.00 to £32,328.00 and cash flow increased by £30,481.00 to £35,344.00.

Please note that, at this point, I did not have to increase sales or implement a new marketing strategy, neither did I have to employ more staff or work longer hours.

This increase in profits and cash flow was the result of simply controlling what is going on within the business: taking the operational side of the company and making it more efficient and lean, cutting out any excess waste and baggage.

Simulation Results

	Past 12 Months	Projected 12 Months	Difference
Sales	248,672	248,672	0
Profit (EBITDA)	19,894	32,328	12,434
Operating Cash Flow	4,863	35,344	30,481

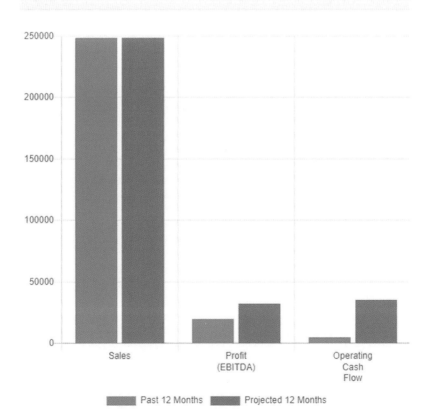

Now that we know the business is operating efficiently and there is a process of converting profit into cash, we can turn our attention to the sixth key in the Cash Flow Code—sales.

What would happen now if sales were to increase by 20%?

Let's take a look: profits would increase by £18,900.00 to £38,794.00. Cash flow would increase by £32,376.00 to £37,239.00.

Simulation Results

	Past 12 Months	Projected 12 Months	Difference
Sales	248,672	298,406	49,734
Profit (EBITDA)	19,894	38,794	18,900
Operating Cash Flow	4,863	37,239	32,376

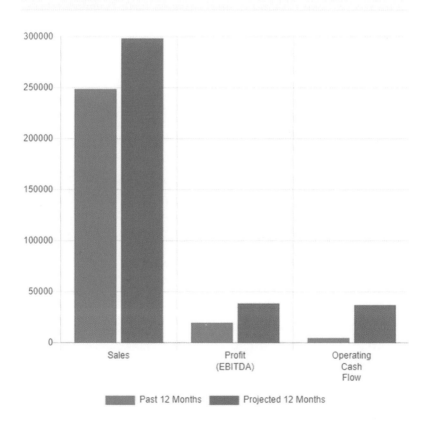

Looking at the two options, which one would you choose?

1. To blindly increase sales by 20% and hope for the best?

2. To first ensure the business is operating as efficiently as possible and then to increase sales by 20%?

Or to put it another way:

1. To increase profits by £3,978.00 and decrease cash flow by £4,202.00?

2. To increase profits by £18,889.00 and increase cash flow by £32,327.00?

Bear in mind that, in both examples, to increase sales by 20%, took the same amount of effort and energy. Therefore, why waste it for a mere £3,978.00 profit and a negative cash flow of £4,202.00 when you could increase profits and cash flow by £18,889.00 and £32,327.00 respectively?

Which Would You Choose?

The most obvious answer, I hope, would be option two—the same amount of effort but a much better yield. Being able to forecast your potential future profits and cash flow will ensure that you not only use your time and energy more productively, it will also help you make better, more strategic decisions—thus reducing your stress levels and putting you in the driver's seat of your business.

This real-life example of using the simulator has illustrated the benefits of running your business with control and efficiency.

As important as it is to use the Cash Flow Simulator to identify key areas within the business that are not working correctly and efficiently, it is equally important to constantly monitor what the cash position is within the business. This vital step in controlling your cash flow will ensure you are prepared for what the future brings and will allow you to always be on the front foot.

In the next and final chapter of this book, we will look at cash flow forecasting and how best to monitor and manage the cash within your business. Proper cash flow management will dramatically reduce stress and ensure you are always prepared for the unforeseen. Let's look at what this looks like on a practical level.

8   CASH FLOW FORECASTING

To RECAP what we have covered so far:

In chapter 2, we looked at the hexagon with its six points that create a well-balanced business. Within this hexagon sit two triangles. The first triangle represents the three unchanging points that make up the fabric of the company: culture, people and resources. And the second triangle represents the three points that reveal the fluidity within the marketplace and the business's ability to adapt to those changes: strategy, systems and execution.

Maximising these six points may take some time to implement and some parts will be ever-evolving as the company grows, changes and adapts to market conditions.

Chapter 3 gave an overview of management accounts—what they are, how they work and how to read them. You may find understanding management accounts very easy, or you may struggle a little. I would encourage everyone to be able to read and understand their company's financials. This will provide you with the optics required to make informed decisions. The more awareness you have and the more informed your decisions are, the more likely you are to get off the rollercoaster of stress and worry and, instead, spend more of your time in control.

Chapter 4 covered assets and expenses and how they impact the business. The goal is to create highly efficient assets whilst reducing expenses as far as possible, without risking quality and service.

In chapter 5, we looked at how to create meaningful data from the three financial statements by calculating ratios that provide you with the necessary trends for monitoring and creating a successful business. Doing this regularly, and over time, allows you to regain and maintain control of your business.

Chapter 6 focused on developing a clear understanding of cash flow. Here, you were introduced to the Cash Flow Code with its six keys that control cash flow. It is vital that you implement these strategies in a way that is suitable for your business. This will allow your business to flourish and for you to create the asset you deserve.

The Cash Flow Simulator was introduced in chapter 7, where a real-life example was given. Through this example, I took you through the steps that I should have taken to prevent the cash-loss that I experienced when running my retail company. The Cash Flow Simulator is a tool that allows you to test and see if your business is ready to grow or if there is anything else you could do to make it even better. Armed with this information, you can implement your plans with confidence and clarity.

Overall, you may find that there are areas within these seven chapters that you will be able to implement immediately and other parts you will adopt over time. There may even be some areas that will require you to invest more time in further research in order to fully understand them. Wherever you are on your business journey, I would urge you to press through any challenges you face, both now and in the future. You don't need to do this alone. Draw on the information available to you: read, listen to the experts and talk to other business owners. This will allow you to become a well-rounded entrepreneur and the best business owner you can be.

If you would like help and support to either overcome or avoid challenges in your business journey, I would be pleased to work with you. Do get in touch at hello@businessoptics.co.uk.

Cash Flow Forecast

So, looking forward... You have now gained a good idea of where your business is heading, your finances are under control, the company is running efficiently and the Cash Flow Simulator is helping to keep everything on track. Now what? What does it all look like on a practical day-to-day level?

In this chapter we will cover the practical side of what you, as a business owner, should be doing to monitor and manage your cash flow using cash flow forecasting.

There are several ways to achieve an accurate cash flow forecast and this is dependent upon the size of your business and budget. With cloud-based accounting, there are some great cash flow forecasting software packages available that will link directly to your accounting software. Alternatively, if you are a small or medium-sized business, you could populate and update the spreadsheet downloadable from www.businessoptics.co.uk/resources.

Whatever your preference or whether you use the free template provided, it is strongly advisable to have a cash flow forecast of some description. In fact, I can't urge you enough.

Populating the Cash Flow Forecast

The way I recommend using a Cash Flow Forecast allows you to see what has happened in the past, what is happening now and what could happen in the future. Knowing what has happened in the past will help you make calculated predictions of what could happen in the future, which is crucial for making the most informed decisions in the present, thus allowing you to maintain real control of your business and staying off that rollercoaster!

When it comes to accurate cash flow forecasting, you will need to work backwards, starting with what you know. The more you break down the information, the more precise your forecast will be.

If you do not yet have a cash flow forecast, I would recommend that you print or export three to six months' worth of bank statements and follow these steps:

The first item you know for certain is the starting balance in your bank account. Place that amount in the blue "Starting Balance" cell towards the bottom of the spreadsheet.

The second section allows you to list all the overheads required for your business to operate and function successfully. Place those figures in the corresponding month, next to the appropriate expense.

If there is an expense that is not listed, please feel free to add or change any items as required. Remember, every business is different and this is *your* cash flow forecast, so please make this spreadsheet your own.

The more detailed you can be, the better. For example, instead of simply having a single line for an expense called "Vehicle Maintenance", maybe you could break it down into "Vehicle Maintenance per Vehicle". If you only have a single row for "Vehicle Maintenance" and there is an increase in this expense, you won't be able to easily identify which vehicle or vehicles are contributing to this increase. Having this clarity enables you to take targeted action quickly and avoid any expenses from getting out of control. It would also allow you to calculate whether replacing certain vehicles would be more cost effective, thus keeping the business as efficient as possible.

Please do this for every expense transaction taken from your bank statement relating to the overhead of your business. If you have not done this before, it may take a little while to input all the details, but it will be worth it. Once it is done, it will simply be a question of keeping it updated on a regular basis.

The following section, cost of goods sold (COGS), mainly applies to product-based businesses, although some service-based businesses could use this as well. Within the payments listed on the bank statement are amounts for cost of goods sold or cost of sales (COGS or COS). These items relate directly to sales of a particular product or service. This will, therefore, need to be listed in the green section, labelled "COST OF GOODS SOLD". Here again, if you can be as accurate and detailed as possible, it will give you better clarity going forward. It is recommended that each product or group of products (if you have several hundred products) are itemised and the corresponding cost for that particular product, service or group is recorded.

The same applies to the last section at the top—the revenue section. Please list all income received in your bank account for that particular month, for that particular product, service or group. Please note, this is not what was invoiced for that month but the money that was received in the bank account.

Please refer to cash vs. accrual accounting in chapter 3 to recap the difference between the two accounting systems.

The cash flow forecast only records the money flowing in and out of your bank account.

Key Formulas

At the bottom of the Cash Flow Forecast, you will find the area where you can input the figures directly from the profit and loss statement and balance sheet account to record the sales, EBITDA, asset value, expenses and cash in the bank for that month.

The key formulas will automatically be calculated for you. You will want each of these numbers to be as optimum as possible with a good trend line. Any trends opposite to the expected result will highlight that a part of your business needs attention.

Forecasting

Sales: sales forecasting should allow you to know your company's marketing plan, lead conversions and financial cycle, i.e., you'll know which months are busy and which months are quiet.

This will allow you to:

1. Predict how many sales you need every month, quarter and year to break even

2. Be aware of how you should manage your cash flow during future quiet periods

3. Highlight any drop in sales, which may cause a cash shortfall at the end of the period

Expenses: most of the company's expenses can be extrapolated across the year, based upon it either being a fixed monthly cost or an accurately predicted figure. Forecasting your expenses allows you to work out your company's financial burn-rate. A burn-rate is the amount of money a business spends every month to keep it solvent.

Using the Cash Flow Forecast Spreadsheet

Now that the spreadsheet is populated with the last three to six months' worth of bank statements, you can predict what will happen to expenses over the next 12 months. You can also calculate how many sales you need, based upon total expenses plus cost of sales.

I recommend that you update this forecast every week or at least every two weeks. I tend to do this on a Friday. This will allow you to update the forecast in real time and make any changes to future figures, be it sales or expenses.

So, as time goes on, you will start to build up a very accurate picture of what you have spent money on, a true monthly view of what you are currently spending money on and an accurate forecast of what you will be spending money on in the future.

By combining this clarity with a comprehensive and detailed marketing plan, you can strategically plan the coming 12 months.

The Four-Account System

Now that you have a handle on your cash flow, it is time to ensure you remain in control. Over the years I have used the four-account system and I strongly recommend you use something similar.

The four accounts work as follows: the first is a current account for all your business activities, where you pay suppliers and receive payments for products or services you provide. The second and third are savings accounts, one account for your profits and the other for all your tax liabilities. The fourth is a commercial credit card. In other words:

Current Account: from which you pay your bills and all operating expenses and receive payments from sales.

Tax Account: remove all cash from the current account designated for all upcoming tax payments, including corporation tax, VAT or any other tax liability that will be due at some point in the future.

Profit Account: if any excess cash remains in the current account, divert this money to the profit account to create a buffer for any unforeseen circumstances. It is a good rule of thumb to always have at least three months' worth of monthly expenses in this account at all times. If you are able to have more than three months' worth of expenses, that would be a bonus.

Commercial Credit Card: having a commercial credit card will enable you to reduce any cash-gaps you may have. It is simply giving you an extra 15 to 30 days to chase sales invoices or make additional cash sales to make up the shortfall. At this point, it is all about protecting the cash flow.

Please Note: this credit card is not to be used as a "loan" facility but only a means of delaying cash from leaving your current account.

Business Account - END of the month

Tax Liability	Profit	Operating Cash Flow

Tax Account - AFTER end of month

Tax Liability	

Profit Account - AFTER end of month

Profit	

Current Business Account - START of the month

Operating Cash Flow	

Using this system will ensure you put profit and certain key liabilities, such as tax and VAT, to one side where you will not be tempted to spend the money, which may be available but, in reality, is not yours to spend. It is such a great feeling to have the money set aside to simply pay off any VAT or corporation tax due because you are not panicking and stressing that you do not have the money to pay it.

In Conclusion

Having a purpose and direction for your business, leading your team from the front and providing the appropriate resources will create stability and cohesion within your company. Being able to adapt your strategy, systems and execution within an ever-changing environment will ensure your business remains current and ahead of the competition.

Understanding your company's finances, improving the efficiencies of income-generating and cost-saving assets, whilst at the same time monitoring the money being spent, will create a highly profitable business.

Using the six keys to ensure that cash flow is under control, by constantly monitoring the main trends addressed in chapter 5 and by using the Cash Flow Simulator tool, you will give your business the best chance of not only surviving but thriving.

Gaining this level of control over all aspects of your business will give you the confidence and financial resources to make the decisions required to grow your business and serve the community in which you operate.

Thank you for taking the time to read The Cash Flow Code. I hope you have found it useful wherever you are on your entrepreneurial journey. Should you have any questions, concerns or you'd like further information and perhaps even assistance in implementing these strategies, please contact me, Cliff, at: hello@businessoptics.co.uk or visit www.businessoptics.co.uk.

I want to wish you the very best and every success for your future.

ABOUT THE AUTHOR

Working with business owners whose companies are at the early start-up phase right through to those with a multi-million pound turnover, Cliff focuses on a wide range of development areas: from organic growth, acquisitions and franchising/licensing, to constructing exit strategies for those business owners looking to retire or progress to other projects.

Outcomes are achieved by ensuring each business has the correct foundations in order to sustain growth in a controlled and organised manner. This includes training, working with staff and board members and creating coherence and focus to achieve the company's goals. In order to ensure a competitive edge, the company's finances, products/services, operations and future developments are analysed and developed to ensure maximum efficiency.

As an ex-military officer, Cliff gained valuable leadership and management skills. He has been trained to adapt and to seek effective solutions in an ever-changing environment. This has formed the backbone of his success in running his own companies for the past 20 years. Throughout this time, he has started, bought, sold, franchised, licensed and systematised several businesses in a variety of sectors.

To learn more about how Cliff could help you grow your business, as well as for more information and additional resources, please visit www.businessoptics.co.uk or email hello@businessoptics.co.uk.

CAN YOU HELP?

Thank You for Reading My Book!

I really appreciate all of your feedback and I love hearing what you have to say.

I need your input to make the next version of this book and my future books even better.

Please leave me an honest review on Amazon, letting me know what you thought of the book, or you can email me at: hello@businessoptics.co.uk.

Thanks so much!

Cliff